Greatest Golden Pieces

Greatest Golden Pieces: Volume 2

Copyright © 2024 by Jean René Bazin PierrePierre. All rights reserved.

No part of this publication may be reproduced, stored in a retrieval system, or transmitted in any form or by any means, digital, electronic, mechanical, photocopying, recording, or otherwise, or conveyed via the Internet or a website without prior written permission of the publisher, except in the case of brief quotations embodied in critical articles and reviews.

BlueInk
SCRIBBLE

Printed in the United States of America

Greatest Golden Pieces

Volume 2

Jean René Bazin PierrePierre

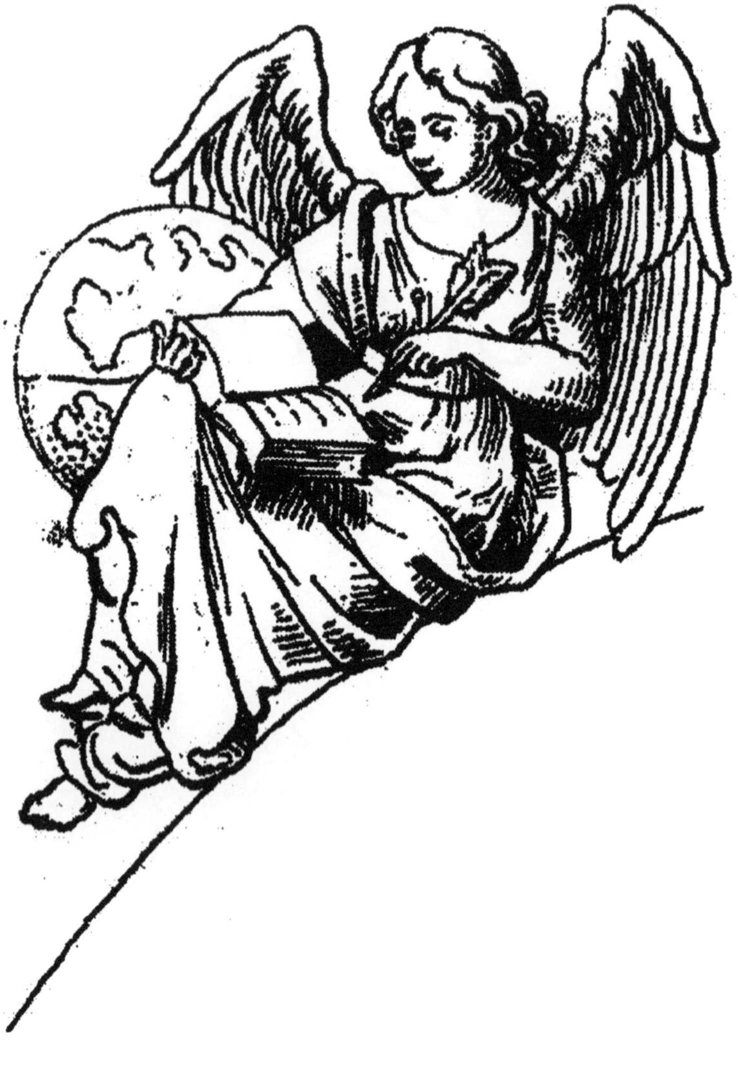

Content

Foreword 1
Preface 3
Recall 4
Suddenly 7
Sorrow street 8
Clearwater Beach Pier. 10
The conscience 15
The pier and I 18
Had it not been for you 19
Mercy, Lord 20
Wild thinking. 21
My Darling 24
No more stumble 25
Ghost of fall 32
Like a flower. 33
Sketching 34
Sing Alleluia 38
My lucky star 40
My love for you 41
Life Goes On 45
What If The Mother Was The Door 47
And the poet prayed. 52
The lions 55
The great spin. 62
The Mother 67
Your Eyes 69
My Lord. 71
Ominous threat 72
Good Old July 76
Blesséd Hope 80
Town Quiesence 82
Turgeau 83
Boaz in slumber 88
Desamor. 92
Love bliss 94
Adoration. 97

Down the road 98
Love refrain 100
…And Christ faced up the tomb 101
After the battle 105
The frog 106
The bed we no more share 113
Star of life 116
Lustation 117
Fierceness 118
Someone like you 119
Frankly Speaking 124
And Then There were None 125
Blesséd day 128
Faith Hope Love 129
Belated Reproach 130
Saint John's Gospel 132
Immaculate Mary 134
Let Christmas be merry 136
Dreadful Way Home 138
The destitutes 140
To the lovely Empress 152
Idling 153
Even There 154
Coward Thoughts 158
Depths of His Mercy 159
Inconsequences 161
The Night HE Was Betrayed 162
Under His Wings 163
Relax 165
Life Choices 166
Along The Way 167
Surrender 168
Stillness 169
The Journey 170
It's Time 172
Calmly 173
No Longer 174
The Ears 176

The Sound of Solitude	178
The Great "I AM"	179
Silent Promise	180
Sacred Heart of JESUS	181
MARY, Mother of Love	182
Prayer to The Immaculate Conception of MARY	184
See	186
Softly And Gently	187
Writing	188
From The Start	189
One Sad Day	191
The Old Square	192
Aftermath	193
O Blesśed FATHER	194
Holy Trinity	195
Psalm 27	196
Advent Antiphon	197
Jesus Christ	198
The Lasting Impression	199
Contemplation	200
The Young Girl	202
An evening, in sowing season	206
Song	207
The hydra	208
Charade	209
The Final Point	211
Wintry Nightfall	214
Bare Ceiling	218
What Does His Love Trigger in You	219
Ode to Erato	221
Never Can Say	224
What a Life	225
Made in Heaven	227
The Tales of The Deep Sea	229
The Being to Have	231
Bless The Lord	232
Veni Creator Spiritus	234
When They're Gone	236

Nothing	237
My Ikigay	238
My Junebug	240
Junedreaming	241
Her song	242
Cherry Love	243
Tween us Two	245
Your Love Song	246
You Again	248
NYC Farewell	250
Morning Stillness	252
In God we trust	254
Deep Inside	257
Eventual emergence	265
Said and done	269
Ask and receive	271
Blind Faith	273
Praise to YOU	274
Tomorrow	276
Divine Patience	278
At my horizon	280
Castaway	284
"Since I Have Now Savored…"	287
Daily retreat	288
Shady Glow	289
Forbidden Treats	291
Summer love	293
Love Poems	295
Promise	297
Devotion	299
She	306
Regrets	308
Spring to Fall	311
Outrage	312
Foolish Mind	313
Madam	314
A Visual	316
The Dawn	317
Ponderings	318

Foreword

Prayer of St Francis

Make me a channel of your peace!
Where there is hatred let me bring your love.
Where there is injury, Your pardon, Lord,
And where there's doubt, true faith in You.

Make me a channel of your peace!
Where there's depair in life let me bring hope,
Where there is darkness, only light.
And where is sadness, ever joy.

O Master, grant that I may never seek
So much to be consoled as to console,
To be understood as to understand
To be loved, as to love with all my soul.

Make me a channel of your peace!
It is in pardoning that we are pardoned,
In giving of ourselves that we receive,
And in dying that we're born to eternal life

Preface

...Therefore inspiration, the work of the Spirit,
Will always reach the ones that it wants to nourish.
Lovingly, stealthily, it leads to the finish
The soul that once chosen, opens up to its treats .

There's never a recess, nor a lack of resource
Since it draws directly all from the divine font.
It glides over heartaches, all miseries affront,
Comes amid any toil, tramples plans on their course.

It flies over frontiers, shuns genders and all race,
Has no times at its clock, never rings any bell.
It shows no preference, any gloom it can quell,
Though rare and much precious, when sought for leaves no trace.

It enlightens us all, ignorant and unread,
Gives places of honor amid dignitaries.
And the load is so light that it asks to carry
That it weighs like feather, and feels light as a thread.

Therefore inspiration, sensing humility,
Will come and crash ashore of the many chosen.
Never has it been said that they were left frozen,
Those who so stealthily receive its verity.

Recall

The supple timbre of your voice
That the silence comes in to chase
Rings on my mind like a sweet noise
And tills the landscape of my face.

Once upon it was melody
That the most skillful of cellist
With golden fingers though sturdy
Would one day ever find the piste.

Once upon at its very sound
As sweet and sassy as can be,
Any worry that was around
Would surely be matched, not maybe.

The supple timbre of your voice
That in my heart left a deep trace
Comes often to make me rejoice
As you come bask in my embrace.

Often life brings its tragedies
Then I'm submerged by daily deeds
But amid all these maladies
Its solace always comes to feed.

There I rejoin the quiescence
That foments the recall of words,
These words uttered for sustainance
For now I live on what's once heard.

The supple timbre of your voice
Will always remain audible,
And stamp my world with content poise
Though now you are unreachable.

But as you're now so far away,
Now that my whole world imploded,
Now that the silence got its way,
All your words my mind downloaded.

And they resound to ease my pain,
They resound like a good old seed
That planted deep within my brain
Gives solace as they slowly feed.

The suppple timbre of your voice
Showers my world with words that fit.
They know they are my unique choice,
They know they are my loving treat.

They come at the rise of the sun
They entertain my loneliness,
They linger as bearer of fun
Till the moon the earth come caress.

And so it went, and so it goes
While my life carries the remnants,
The remnants of love that echoes
And just won't die while I lament.

The supple timbre of your voice
Declares out loud my love for you.
It attests that there's no more choice,
That I'll be yours my whole life through.

Suddenly

Suddenly, in life it nudges
Just ignoring one's surroundings,
Suddenly, appeasing grudges,
Love in our hearts makes a landing.

Suddenly now we are speechless,
Suddenly hung to a bright smile.
Suddenly, it is so priceless,
Suddenly it was worth the while

That we waited so long to see
These eyes in which our sun rises,
This face revealing God's mercy,
As if His mercy had sizes.

But suddenly the elation,
The heart racing, the sweaty palms,
The dry mouth, verbal confusion,
Love has landed with its sweet balm.

Suddenly, like no déjà vu,
She is the queen of your palace,
Suddenly, right in your purview,
All your plans you gladly replace.

To my sister, Jacotte

Sorrow street

In this small house of Sorrow street,
Around the table we all sit,
Gathered to have our dinner treats,
My dear sister, but you are gone.
The pain lingers in every heart
Since that day you chose to depart,
That grief in us planted its dart,
Of your kind words now we hear none.

Why did you have to go so soon?
You had our love, O dearest boon,
We no longer can hear you croon,
For sadly with us you're not there.
The pain that you so long carried,
You stoically never varied,
You always gay, always merry,
To everyone showed tender care.

You gladly chose our parents stance.
Sadly we did not stand a chance,
Over us they had preference,
So you crossed to their side of shore.
In Sorrow street, that house so bleak,
Your presence everywhere yet sticks,
Your soothing words everyone seeks,
Their sounds lull us deep in the core.

The kids took a damaging blow,
The best auntie they had to show,
All crushed under debris below.
O my sister, what an anguish!
And suddenly what emptiness!
What heavy load on every chest!
Each one silently does his best
But we all miss the so cherished.

Thalie will move on. She is strong.
She carries well her sorrow prongs.
Well imbued of what's right or wrong
She'll go forward as half orphan.
May the good Lord show clemency,
And enfold you in His mercy
So to relieve our poignancy.
To Him all pray'rs and shows of hands.

Clearwater Beach Pier

(Summer Eve)

The crimson sky of late July
In the air puts an eerie touch.
You see late birds here and there fly
To finish errands in a rush.

Relentless waves with foamy crowns
Come crashing gainst the wooden pier
Whose moldy beams don't give a frown;
Their shoving, they no longer fear.

The golden sand now dark and gray
Still retains traces of the crowd.
The many bodies that here lay
Left echoes that are much too loud.

There you can see the tall hotel
Hugging its frontal part of sand.
There a small crowd tries not to quell
The noise of their half naked band.

A few lovers go hand in hand
With feet in the foamy waters.
While happy tods dance to the band
Whose rhythm they seem to falter.

The palm trees welcome the cooling
Now that the sun is far away.
They stand erect, so imposing,
Standing its heat day after day.

The merchants gathered on the pier
Begin repacking unsold goods
While others profit of the mere
Occasions to open their hoods.

The ice cream parlor's still open
To young girls and their families,
And young boys who return often
To skateboard while keeping tallies.

The sea birds you no longer see
Took part at this afternoon feast.
They ate, swooping with no mercy,
Of human beings afraid the least.

And patiently, and patiently
The fishermen hold to their bait.
They hang as on a balcony,
Pond'ring over their dinner fate.

But often their concentration
Is broken by the quick surging
Of a jet sky strong pulsation
To its dock safely returning.

If suddenly you hear a scream,
Sign of random successful catch,
It gives the rest of them, it seems,
Some hope for a much longer watch.

The band had long taken a break.
The surf's now roaring loud and clear.
A little girl cries her heartache,
From the water she was too near.

So in the arms of her mother
She gesticulates a tantrum.
Before I could see her laughter
Now I see the frown of her mum.

Those two remaining on the sand
Seem to ignore the passers-by.
They don't see those they may offend,
They don't, while on the sand they lie.

And suddenly you get to see
The lights of Tampa Bay by night
Glittering the indigo sea,
A genuine delight to the sight.

Closer to me a proud old man
Displays his catch of the evening,
A feisty trout whose dinner plan
Just became the old man's feeding.

And the band resumes its vacarm,
And the crowd their dirty dancing.
And this young lady full of charm
Can't even hear her cellphone ring.

A rugged young man is upset
At the gate keeper of the pier,
The change he put just could not get
To work the turnstile, it appears.

*So louder, longer they argue
Till finally some other guy
Offers the quarter overdue
For him who hurriedly zooms by*

*Rushing to the end of the pier
Bringing to his other pana
What could as well have been a beer,
Forbidden on the marina.*

*And the darkness made its entrance
Robed in a gown of shiny stars,
By then the crowd got in a transe
Caused by the "Island Superstars".*

*And so it came, and so it went
This Saturday of late July.
A few teens came folding the tents,
Helping this older, skinnier guy.*

*What then to do, what, tell me please,
What else to savor, the weather?
Seventy-nine lovely degrees,
A gorgeous evening, my brother!*

The conscience

Donned with skins of wild beasts, disheveled and livid,
With mate and brood in tow, crushed under his dark deed,
When Cain ran in hiding, shunning the face of God,
At the fall of the day, the fallen man so trod

From a lofty mountain, down this arid valley,
His wife all exhausted, sons walking languidly,
Begged to him: "Let's just lie, right on the ground and rest."
Cain, somber, with no sleep, pondered devoid of zest.

Looking up to the sky all gloomy and somber,
He saw the all-seeing Eye, piercing his thought chamber,
Looking so steadily down to his very core.
"I'm yet too close", he thought, disturbed, shaking some more.

So he woke up his sons, his wife, lost and weary,
And so kept on fleeing through dark territory.
He pressed on thirty days, he pressed on thirty nights,
All mute, pale, shivering, drowning in inner fright,

Sneakily, straight ahead, without a break he spanked,
Restlessly, sleeplessly, till he reaches the bank
Of the sea of the land known since then as Assur.
"Let us stop here, he said, for this place is secure.

Let's stay here and settle. We reached the world border."
And as he sat, weary, caught glance, high and yonder,
Of the Eye in the sky, deep at the horizon.
He shuddered all perturbed, beyond well-known reason.

"Hide me now!" he shouted; and perplexed to the bones,
All his sons stood looking at the Eye fierce and honed.
Cain then said to Jabel, father of those who dwell,
Deep within the desert, under tents that winds swell:

"Spread out on this side the large veil of the tent."
They opened up the skin, as it was the intent,
When it was all steadied, anchored with weights of lead,
"Do you still see something?" said Tsilla, of tears fed,

From seeing her elder so frazzled and flurried,
But Cain replied freaked out: " I still see it. Hurry!"
Jubal, father of those who wonder in boroughs,
Blowing horns on their ways and beatings drums in row,

Shouted: "I will erect then one of these rampart."
He built a wall on bronze just to put Cain apart.
And Cain said: "This keen Eye right at me again peers!"
Enoch said: "We must build a tall cloister right here,"

"So tall that nothing will bother its strong towers.
Let's build up a whole town, with great might and power,
Yeah, let's erect a town and then close its border."
Then Tubal-Cain, the one who blacksmiths, engender,'

Constructed a big town, immense and powerful.
And as he was working, his brothers all zestful,
Chased away Enos' sons and every Seth's offspring,
Tearing out the eyeballs of the ones defying,

And bedazzled at night, shot arrow at the stars.
And the stonewall replaced the tents of veil and tar,
With stones held together by nods of crude metal
And the town would favor a park bleak and bestial,

Everywhere the tall walls would cast shadows galore
Turning the least tower into an arm that'd soar.
And on the door was carved: "God is not allowed here".
Thus they walled and cloistered their deep, encrusted fear.

Then deep in the middle, behind towers of stones,
Haggard and sinister, Cain was placed, as he groan'.
"Do you still see the eye?" Asked Tsilla, in quivers.
And Cain squealed: "Yes my dear, bury me!" He shiver'.

"Just like a lifeless corps, just put me underground,
Well hidden from all sight, where I'll never be found".
And they dug a deep hole that was just as he said.
He planned to go inside and securely be laid.

So he went down the pit, under a somber vault,
There, in the dark chamber, just as dark as his fault,
He reclined in despair, but still within this den,
The Eye, there in silence, kept looking right at Cain.

The pier and I

The shade of sand, the rank of fish
Overtly lurking in the air,
Amid July nonchalant pairs
Showcasing their cheap love affairs
In this landscape they so cherish.

Alone in the midst of my sighs
Let me decline the lucid thoughts
Raking my soul while I'm still caught
In this lament that I long fought,
But like the tide, is now knee high.

Had it not been for you

Had it not been for you, through the thick and the thin,
Through my every season: spring, summer, winter, fall,
Had it not been for you, the voice of every call,
Will I be standing here with all this love within?

Had it not been for you, from the very get go,
Who polished the image of my deep wounded soul,
Who rekindled that flame of love story of old
And fine-tuned my poor heart to yours steady echo?

Had it not been for you, with shoulder wet from tears,
Tears shed through the seasons, the friends, the boos, the wives,
Disheartening failures, gut-wrenching inner strives,
Would there be this angel to chase away my fears?

Had it not been for you, the hero of my dreams,
Who quenched all my fires set up by all the foes,
Who dispelled the distress of my slighted ego,
Would there be a soul mate to silence all my screams?

But it's been only you, my love, my angel fine,
My faithful companion, my well-hidden treasure,
My source of love divine, the dew of my nature.
It's only for your love that from now on I pine.

Mercy, Lord

When I am alone and sad
And around me the world's gone mad.
When I feel I will not make
The many plans I undertake.

If I feel too big my pride
Though my sorrow I cannot hide.
When the pain is much to bear,
Not even a smile I can wear.

When I try to make amend
For your sweet Face I did offend
For I failed to lend a hand
At my neighbor's pressing demand.

And if I kneel down and pray,
From my cry Lord, don't turn away.
I will wait, O my Savior,
Your forgiveness will not falter.

Wild thinking

I see it irks listening
To my rants with line so bleak
And the words of my rhyming
Though you know well what they seek
Fail to nudge your stark thinking.

Never has it been a trend
Living in these nowadays
With all mores that this world bends
To ask that the human prays,
Fear of neighbors to offend.

What I now hold in esteem
To my mate is obsolete
I just cannot make it seem
Upholding what she sees fit
To be pursued as a dream.

I'll never, I know I tried,
To change or dilute the truth,
Make believe or just plain lie
See the slaughtering of sooth
And calmly keep a blind eye.

Whoever gospel contorts
Either for pride or just greed
Or afraid of clear retort
So from their conscience to speed
In detrimental effort

Is bound to bawl and grind teeth
Left stranded in sheer mire
For no teaching should one sieve
Holy Ghost not to tire
And thus the brethren deceive.

Away from me then depart
And go hang out with hip crowds.
They do not follow their heart
But rather feel very proud
Of their most vile inner parts.

Crosses are sown all over
When carried you get merits
Needed for safe crossover
As combo soul and spirit
Sheds off their carnal cover.

The world tends to become one
The borders slowly fading
Alllegiance they claim to none
Everyone who's suffering
Has crown of thorns and a throne.

Meanwhile deep, deep within me
I guard safely the strong hope
Fueling dreams ever stormy
That they clash and fail to cope
With Heavens pink and balmy.

Therefore what I say I say
As I throw my net to sea
I will have yea or have nay
But I pray one day you see
That as I write so I pray.

You'll go clamor word misuse
Look for ways to shut me down
The semantics I abuse
Come trickling down from the frown
Of the one I call my muse.

First poem to Junie, 1/28/1997

My Darling

Just wanted to tell you how sweet your embrace feels
And how holding you close marveled me to the chills.
The magic of the Bay, the sweet peace of your room
Made that last Sunday night ecstatic, free of gloom.

I had to be away from what I so treasure
To swear not to ever refrain from such pleasure.
You made me feel so new, so warm and so alive
That I declare aloud that you're my better half.

I love you my darling, and for so strong reasons
That I often wonder why do I stay alone.
But to rush is to fail, nothing is finalized
Unless it is over and over analyzed.

So darling, we'll get there though again we may face
Either tougher rival or even bigger mace.
Enough, I said enough, let me just end my rhyme
With the sweet taste I have of getting back my prime.

No more stumble

For the very first day you crashed into my life
You magically just quelled my every single strife.
I followed you blindly,
And loved you so kindly
That in a quite short time you had become my wife.

But soon I discovered that you were but a fake
For from you I received nothing but sheer heartache.
Nothing lasts for ever,
But I swore to never
Go again and repeat such a foolish mistake.

Life with us plays its game but often what we get
Marks us deep in the core, and we just can't forget,
For taken so aback,
We get shoved off our track,
Bruised up and sore as though we were wounded target.

I invested my all, never thought you'd fail me.
You promised everything to the trusting dummy
Wrapped around your finger.
You became the stinger
And my heart fell stricken under this infamy.

But for the life of me, I swore you were the one
You did everything right, not an act was undone.
You knew all the right moves
My perturbed mind to soothe
Until the wretched time when feelings you had none.

We tried all kind of help, you went along with it,
Blaming it all on stress, you so shrewd and so fit
When your coldness swan dove
It came my heart to shove
And right between our souls, calmly it took a seat.

I remembered your words, recalled all your gestures
Which made it all tougher your new stance to endure
But at every clear dawn
Like a baffled, sad pawn,
Pitifully I'd hope for some brighter future.

But the years came and went, but nothing in you changed,
You simply left my world, grew steadily estranged.
We ceased to be a pair,
For this ill love affair
Had retired your smile and all plans rearranged.

So life for us went on, each one living his own.
I had nowhere to go since my heart you disowned,
But you followed your plan,
Knew quite well where to stand,
You stood there for sometimes, glowing in the unknown.

But through all I carried from your bold change of heart
The worst showed up after, tore mine into small parts.
Never saw it coming,
But you went on wiling,
It was a risk taken by the ones way too smart.

Twas blow below the belt but it was your best shot,
It hit in broad daylight, got me so much distraught
That even your close friends
Stepped in to put an end
To what they all saw as something no one would sought.

When I look at it now, now that it's all behind,
I somewhat feel releived but it dwells on my mind
That one can never tell
They know any one well.
Brace yourself for the worst, but in all remain kind.

To any one who'd ask, I'd answer them the same,
That's what life's all about, that no one is to blame,
That in spite of all this,
That some call cowardice,
I won't harbor hatred or behaving with shame.

For early I was taught that whatever you sow,
Acts of gentle kindness or deceit in a row
Before it is too late,
You receive on your plate
The same vibes you sent out with gloomy greif in tow.

Whereas what is suffered in blessed tolerance,
In turn pours over you your share of recompense,
In bundle as He says,
On your laps it will lay
For the whole world to see, and they won't call it chance.

For losers of this world are never true losers.
They appear as failures compared to the others,
But what they seem to lack
One day will swing right back,
And all over their world sow blessings in showers.

Oh yes you left and went your bright and merry way,
Yes I stayed there choking on all that I could say.
I bid you true farewell,
It's all that I could tell
Though deep inside I wish you would not go away.

But the fate that befalls the average human being
Comes swiftly upon him, his plans, readjusting.
It bursts one sunny day,
Spreads its load of dismay,
Rearranging his world with no hint, no warning.

The turmoil that ensues is never déjà vu.
It comes with a program and knows well its purview.
It comes lessons to teach,
It comes stressing on each
And every blunt aspect, spreading grief and sinew.

The subject it ensnares will always resurface
In the world he resides with a rose or a mace.
A rose, to spread more love,
Mace, with hatred to shove
Every one around him and with bitterness lace.

Stressors in this here life bring out of us the best.
The true self will emerge revealing the deep chest.
The bitter one will rage,
The meek one will be sage.
This always takes effect at the end of all tests.

But always from above is given the free will,
The will to please the light or pamper hatred still.
Regardless of the blow,
Regardless of how low,
What you give in return, your true nature reveals.

Misery well carried brings about blessed things.
When mishandled it pours calamities in strings.
It's the offered solace
To the ones who truce chase
When despite all efforts only pure grief life brings.

And they press on knowing that better days will come,
And they press on hoping on the blessed Kingdom
That will arrive for sure
For it is well ensured
By the One whose Spirit enlightens, the Awesome.

And yet in spite of all life keeps its steady course.
Regardless of failures do not craddle remorse.
A clean slate is offered
To the soul who suffered
And can offer his pain for some spiritual bourse.

This trade is feasible at just every level
For the soul always gains when the body snivels.
It rises and ascends
And joyfully transcends,
Nearing hidden treasures to the sight unravel'.

But we pamper one self, stepping on everyone.
Despite the "Thou shall not" no one spares any one.
The world karma's tarnished.
True love has long vanished
From every human heart where it once gladly shone.

Everyone claims the right to bear their deepest stains
Right out on their sleeve, to their neighbor's expense.
Everything is allowed,
Everything is avowed
And all this just baffles even the common sense.

So went my reflexion, all alone in the dark,
As I drown in sorrow on this stage grim and stark.
All the wisdom you gained
Failed to help you retain
The peace within your soul that now left a sad mark.

If I survive this blow, the Spirit is able,
I will not once again suffer such a stumble.
Life to us can be kind
But yet we ought to mind
The stones on this journey. The heart's no more nimble.

I'll take my load of grief as it was sent to me
But for now will steer clear of any infamy.
Though crushed and downtrodden
I will stay in this den,
Will not go entertain any kind of gamy.

But yes, when I saw her, I thought of lucky star,
But little did I know I had found one that chars.
Now all scorched up I stand,
But now I understand
No more stumble for me, I have my share of scars.

Ghost of fall

Spirit of fall, Autumn leaves cover your demise,
To infuse in all our hearts blessed hope.
Ghost, mournful to the eyes,
Convey to us all
Pledges of the fall.

Spirit of fall, enchant us with your magic shades,
To enliven the world, your vast domain,
Caught in your leaf parade
Sustain deep within us
A sense of trust.

I offer you tears of all broken hearts,
All sufferings muffled by your leaves,
I bring to you all lovers torn apart,
Walking your streets, hearts upon sleeves.

Here at your feet, I commit my sorrow,
The joys of old, all hopes deeply fondled.
Winter awaits, ghost of fall will you blow
Far, far away all pain carried in bundle.

Like a flower

Like a flower you come adorn
The bleak and somber world of mine.
By the others it has been scorned
But you came and it gladly shines.

Like a flower you come dispense
Your aroma of love and care
That trickles and changes this tense
And stressy landscape all so bare.

Your jokes and laughter then recoil
Stroking the walls of my chamber
Where quietly I char and toil
With my psyche calm yet somber.

Like a flower sprinkle your dew
Over the dryness of my land
My parched lips tremble as we two
Cuddle, cuddle in loving trend.

Like a flower therefore remain
With bright petals and long, slim stalk.
Be my angel, I'll be your man
And freely we'll let our hearts talk.

Sketching

I sit alone amid the sound
Of thoughts running wild on my mind
They run like kids on open ground,
Run leaving my hearbeats behind.

They run pass the cemetery
Where lie slaughtered the dreams we made
They run afraid of the eerie
Glow emerging from the tomb shades.

Lack of vigor or lack of zest
I just don't feel up to the chase.
They drown the beating in my chest
For you age as you stay in place.

But then now come unknown faces
Some come smiling, some rather not
They fly living shadow traces,
They fly for they see me distraught.

Then I contemplate better days
Where nightingales would come along
To make amend for my dismay,
Bring solace needed for so long.

All compell me to write and write
So I can dispel this mistruth.
As Sunday to the week is light
As clear hope is to blessed truth.

But let it be, just let it be,
Let it on my mind wreak havoc.
Give my wackineess this freebie,
To my thoughts don't put any block.

Long, long ago I had a plan,
A plan solid as a refrain
But when in me this came to land
Pure ravage beset my poor brain

Which for a while went on idling
Leaving my body vegetate
While the whole world went on living
Moved by my being and its state.

Then I return to my tableau
Well aware of what is at stake,
So not to interrupt the flow
Of these thoughts coming loose but fake.

Always when carrying a cross
Willfully one forsakes the rest
And on the road where grows no moss
All flowers have long lost their zest.

But love in the midst of it all
In its splendor blots every flaw.
From all tree tops you hear the calls
Of white doves with roses in claw.

What is offered to me as balm
Never had any worth in pence.
It has been the cheapest of palms
For those deprived of common sense.

This chaos that seems to bring peace
Rings in my ears rendered now deaf.
But my mind still fails to dismiss
This havoc that has never left.

But breathe and breathe, expell the heat
Caused by this damage of psyche.
Bring down, bring down your rate of beats,
This heart witnessed scenes too freaky.

And every time comes a new song
Deemed to upset my inner peace
It comes ringing so vile and strong
That each dawn I hope this would cease.

But the sun with its heat persists
Leaning heavy gainst the windows
So bright that shadows lose their pistes
And run hide into deep furrows.

But as I lose my sanity
Wrapped in folds of my common sense
What I spit in audacity
I used to call it pure nonsense.

Meanwhile alone I sit and watch
Faces, shadows and deafening sounds,
As they descend, a scary batch
Set to distabilized my ground.

Lack of vigor or lack of zest,
Soon all this will have a meaning.
I'll focus on passing the test
That so far has kept me dreaming.

Sing Alleluia

Give thanks, give thanks to Him, our Lord.
He gives what we can't afford.
His love for us knows no boundary,
He longs to show us His Mercy.

So many times we hear His call
But many times we fail and fall,
But He, the merciful Father,
Forgets His creatures but never.

He gives us his mighty Spirit
Which our poor nature does complete.
Throughout our life He sustains us
That in His eyes we remain just.

He repeatedly when we pray
Strenghtens us in all our dismay,
And lovingly stands us steady
Amid our own sin misery.

So many times He gives us sight
Of his great Love, Power and Might
But senselessly we come up short
Of His truth we often contort.

So now sing praises to our God.
Give thanks to the Almighty Lord.
Towards us He shows His kindness
And gives us lots of His richness.

Then make a testimony leap
For if a king's treasure's to keep
The work of God we should declare,
With the whole world His graces share.

My lucky star

Rolling stone with no moss,
Heading straight for my loss,
Tossed around here and there as the wind blows.
I'd go from ecstasy
To darkened misery
But one day in my eyes I saw a glow
It was you, my lucky star.

Twas a dim yet steady gleam high above my pit
But it shone so steadily,
Shone so merrily,
And from this instance if I am back on my feet,
It's cause I have your soft light
Always there in my sight.

You enliven my world,
You glitter like a pearl,
And you sing lovingly through every chore.
And like the dearest prize
I set on you my eyes,
And I'm happy unlike ever before
Following my lucky star.

Now I rest so peacefully all through the seasons
Clinching deep within my soul
What now makes me whole,
And when they come inquire, I hide the reason
Why the glow of your soft light
Makes my world gay and bright.

My love for you

The love of you keeps me alive,
Giving me my every day drive.
The love of you keeps me ensnared
Right in the dungeon of your heart,
Your heart that's needed to jump start
My heart stalling without your care.

The love of you gives me strong wings
To bear my lot of sufferings,
Those which describe my state of mind,
My mind where your name wreaks havoc,
Though it's I who live on to stalk
The souvenirs you left behind.

The love of you I so cherish
Saddles me like some strong hashish.
There, all I see are your brown eyes,
That shine as pair of guiding lights.
And I, the bedazzled fawn, fight
To hug their trail deep in my skies.

I sit around on any day
Raving over the thoughts you bring.
It's always the most pleasant thing,
When your spirit deigns come my way.

The love of you gives no warning.
It tramples any happening
With thoughts one just would not think of.
It reigns over body and soul
And naturally has all control
And all matters, suddenly shoves.

The love of you, if I resist,
Resorts to get me off my piste.
So there I stand or rather hang,
Trying then to desparately fake
A facade my mind did not stake,
Like in an internal harangue.

The love of you is God given,
All my wants it comes to even.
It soothes aches, fills up misses,
Always fostering pleasant dreams
That stand loudly in smothered screams,
Revealing spiritual kisses.

It has the span of a lifetime.
It brands what it sees as its prime,
Gently rockabies the spirit,
Where it lives on, as its best treat.

The love of you knows no season,
It performs way beyond reason,
The living heart enlivening,
Giving it strength for one more beat,
The beats that arise as sees fit
The Maker of all living things.

The love of you seems to obsess
But rather it performs to bless
My soul from within which it basks.
At any given time it calms,
And to my desires gives alms
As I tread among daily tasks.

The love of you takes me to shores
Of isles I never knew before.
It makes me glide upon the wings
Of fierce eagles. Over wind blasts
They soar above what overcasts
The sun and its natural bling.

Through ups and downs and come what may
It thrives like buds in month of May
Though in the ears of the many
It sounds like a fake symphony.

The love of you is my banner
That I wave in bravely manner
Each time I face the wicked foe,
The one tripping my every stride
On this journey where we all ride
On whatever mean we may know.

The love of you sheds joyful tears
For through it all it has no fear.
It has lasted its span of time
And stands assured that its future,
Based on its past, is well secured
By the Word of the great I AM.

But since I know you love me too
For God always makes dreams come true
For the ones who crosses carry,
I daily give thanks and praises.
The few that this love amazes
Will be baffled when we marry.

The Lord backs up His promises
With subtle hints no one else sees.
Foolish would we be if ever
We'd go gamble our forever.

Life Goes On

We toddle down the streets of life
Then comes the time when we mature
And deal with all that live's so rife
Till we're crushed by Mother Nature,
And as we feel her every prong
We try to mind the right and wrong
For no matter what life goes on.

The years follow like the seasons,
Nothing lasts long under the sun.
Nature puts a show all day long
But the night seems to offer none.
But in this Earth's merry-go-round
Where joys and miseries abound
At every sunrise life goes on.

Each one has an el dorado
That daily he attempts to reach
And through all acts of bavado
Battles till he gets to its niche.
As he grasps it, as it all seems
They come wake him up from his dream,
But he resets, and life goes on.

The most valued of all the days
Are the ones when love comes to town.
It comes rearrange all our ways
Then leaves us a pitiful frown
For as it stands nothing does last
Though some of us clench to the past
But still placidly life goes on.

And friends will come, and friends will go
In equal sharing as we hope,
But later we hear their echo
As we slowly go down the slope,
But the solace they often bring
Offsets the dread of their cold sting
But yet stoically life goes on.

Through fears and hope we live this life
Though we try to hope more than fear
For steadily at every strife
The Spirit in us helps us steer.
To all needs the Father attends,
Dull is he who this truth, contends
For from the Spirit life goes on.

And sudenly we cease to walk
The surface of this God's green Earth.
We get invited to go stalk
Greater things on God's divine turf.
As this earthly life is no more
Spirit and soul to Heaven soar,
There truly, freely, life goes on.

What If The Mother Was The Door

From the dawning shades of all times,
When there was but the Great I AM,
Your blessed name, bright and lowly,
Shone like the sun over the earth
For the Fruit of your precious girth,
God's handmade, O Virgin Mary!

Conceived to offset the downfall,
Willingly you answered the call
That resonated deep in you.
You were tailor made, the purest
And grace on you shine at its best,
Mother of a race made brand new.

You were thought of and realized
Even before Eve was chastised
For God sees time in all its scope.
So the first couple had its trial
But failed, causing the big downfall
That set the stage for mending hope.

So when God's plan fully matured
You shone in your perfect nature
And played your part most lovingly.
You opened up the earthly door
And like it's never done before,
The Creator trod earth humbly.

He came with love to redirect
His creatures lost, week and abject,
Kept in slavery under sin yoke.
They had managed by their doings
To upset the Supreme Being;
Spirits panting under flesh cloak.

So you receive the Spirit's Seed
Sent up this crumbling world to feed,
Light to shine through the earth darkness.
Beacon to lead on this journey
Done by the brethren, the many,
Created by God sheer goodness.

So He came in a poor manger,
Cold, dark like a common stranger,
The perfect Lamb of sacrifice.
Meek, humble although Almighty,
Obeying those whom He pities,
For thirty years honing the prize.

Often when lost in confusion
We should observe the foe's actions
For they lead to the most precious.
When the dark angel split the church,
Well aware of her divine touch,
He removed her most glorious.

For she's the mother most holy,
The precious gift from Calvary,
Bequeathed by the Font of wisdom,
Who knowing well her depths of heart,
Before He did from us depart
Put His brethren in her bosom.

After He paid for our freedom
By being most worthy ransom
He gave forgiveness and mercy.
And despite all the prongs and thorns
Still full of love yet so much scorned
He poured on us His clemency

For the Virgin did not need us,
She could have been assumed for thus
Was her role on this earth all done.
Just like Her Son through suffering
She had, through life of sword piercing,
Co-redeemed her race of its wrongs.

She had her Son but was assured
How much suffering she would endure,
Always humbly meditating
On what for Him life had in store
And silently the Mother bore
This dim future though God trusting

Yet through her life's daily toiling
She never ceased her pondering
Over what tomorrow will bear.
She is Mother to her lone Son
With love stirring like you've seen none,
Who'd quickly die His life to spare.

But no one will ever fathom
If I write now till kingdom come
The depths of love they had for realm,
They need not to communicate,
Through glance they could all modulate.
Their hearts the same prongs overwhelm'.

She was there in most everything,
When her sweet glance could solace bring,
Prompted His start, stood by His end.
When He completed His great task,
When was done what His Father asked,
She received her Lamb in her hands.

From any son you can gather
That when suffering, they'd much rather
Not have their mother as witness.
Nothing to them is more painful
Than mother's face all sorrowful,
Enduring sword-piercing distress.

Her heart was pierced beyond compare,
Yet she stood there with loving stare,
Offering Her love upon God's Throne
For the rabid stain of our fall,
For ransom demanded her All,
For there He hung, her flesh and bone.

See, the Spirit overshadowed
And the Word was flesh here below
But no gonad set was produced.
The Flesh and Blood that were slaughtered
Came from one source sin-unbothered.
The pure Virgin divinely spruced.

Nobody will ever fathom
The bond divine, beyond awesome
Between the Mother and the Son
And it's fitted that as a Queen
She oversees all divine scenes
As ladies of the house have done.

Yes Peter was given the key,
What he decrees, Heaven agrees.
The Lord set it this way afore.
But for His Mother's love, rightly
Who co-redeemed all so humbly,
He made her of Heaven the door.

And the poet prayed…

Serene and placidly, spreading over the vale
The night smothers the day and the owl shouts the tale.
A light breeze gently rocks baby birds on their hays,
The flowers seem to miss the caress of sunrays.
The lonely mocking bird, unfaithful in its ways
Seems to want to repent for its so many preys.
Even the air you breathe seems dainty to inhale
For placid and serene night falls over the vale.

I cherish these moments of calm and peaceful rest
When everyday voices from within weary chest
Decrease in decibels to die down in silence…
There my soul opens up, recalls its provenance.
At these painful hours summing all miseries,
When the world introspects arousing all queries
And the joys of the day have magically faded,
Simply I relinquish to these hours shaded
Peacefully invading the muffled surroundings
There Your Love permeates the core of every being,
Revealing Your goodness when the day expires.
Just like in Your heaven You ignite Your fires,
Enkindle in the hearts, O my Lord, Your Spirit…

On my knees I implore Your loving clemency
For the so many hearts ignoring Your Mercy.
Caught in the carnal world of making a living
You, the Source of all lives, they go daily missing.
I beseech You, my Lord, for the ones who feel shame
When the world proudly japes for they call on Your Name.
Lord, You always raise up the meek and the lowly
While for fleeting power this here world raves only.
To love and to serve You seem a waste of one's time,
So great many of us ignore the divine chime
Reminding the creatures to heed the Creator.

I beg for Your Mercy, O most loving Savior,
For the brokenhearted, for the withering soul,
In Your loving kindness, have pity, make them whole.
For the wandering kind, the ones who lost all hope,
Who became hard and cold, those who no longer mope.

Lord I also offer the narcissistic one
Who linger in the mire of loving self alone,
Caught in the dreary links of egotistic net
While loving his neighbor would change the world facet.
O Lord I pray also for the cold murderer
Who often repudiates the baptismal marker
That you give Your children as spiritual sticker.

For the sign of these times is that at early age
The sparrow of candor flees from the young child's cage,
And divine innocence, the key to happiness,
Cannot release the flow of the graces that bless
The heart who lovingly upholds all of Your laws.
So they go on marching, claiming rights for their flaws,
Drearily they become true spiritual outlaws.

O Master, remind them of Your plan the detail,
That Love alone matters and will always prevail,
For the least of the deeds done unto Your brethren
Your justice will always come make matters even.

The lions

There, in the somber pit, famished and held captive,
The lions roared aloud, by nature so deceived,
For if every creature is fed under its dome,
They, lions were starving and salivating foam.

For three long days they roared, frothed of red hungry rage,
Peering through the strong bars, down from their muddy cage,
To see yet one more dusk in the crimson azure.
Their growl pierced the heavens, shaking every creature

Roaming the horizon over the blazing hills.
They fanned their tail to soothe that part they could not fill.
And the walls of the trench trembled at each howling
For the hungry lions from their pangs were roaring.

The fossa was so deep for it was hewn mainly
By Og and his big sons, so they could hide safely.
Those children of the land had built in their intent
That colossal palace from this rocky descent.

Their heads had burst open right through the somber dome
And sunlight would come in, bringing life from the gloam.
And this dreaded dungeon would gape to the azure.
King Nebuchadnezzar, ruler of the Assur,

Had made built a cover over the opening
And he had made usage, as a true tawny king,
Of what once used the Chams and the Deucalions,
And built to suit giants, a true den for lions.

They were four and dreadful. A litter of dry bones
Covered the muddy ground for those beasts anger prone.
Rocks of mighty stature poured shadows over them
And they walked while breaking on the ground bony stems,

Stepping on carcasses and skeletal remains.
The first one ruled over the arid Sodom plains.
Once upon in its prime, in its tawny freedom,
It roamed the old Sinai, reigned mighty and lonesome,

In deafening silence and kingly solitude.
Woe to whosoever would fall under the rude
Hair of its mighty paws, facing its sturdy stand,
Once upon, not so long, strong lion of the sand.

The second one came from the Euphrates forest.
When it'd come down potent, roaming the river crest,
All would run. Catching him was no walk in the park,
Packs of two kings, with loads of nets and barks,

It roared loud for it was a lion of the woods.
The third one, in mountains, that's where its kingdom stood.
Yore, lingering shadows and horror paved its way.

At that time, when you'd hear, down from muddy gulches,
The desperate stampede all under the branches,
Of herds, warriors, shepherds and all pastors alike,
All running for their lives, then you'd see its head spike.

The forth and last monster, appalling and so proud
Was a seashore lion, roaming under the clouds.
It drifted the sea bank right before its capture,
Gur, strong city of then, was born of this tenure.

Smoky rooftops, with docks loaded with various ships,
Whose masts giving a clue of their nature of trips,
The peasant carrying his satchel full of goods
Would go there; the prophet brought his spiritual food.

They were happy people, like on tree branches birds.
Gur had a lovely square, a market full of herds,
And the Abyssinian would trade his ivory,
The Amorrite would bring amber and hickory,

Ascalonian, butter, of Abha, the good wheat.
The town remained busy from the flow of its fleet.
This town activity troubled this great lion,
And at night, all alone, weighing its intention,

Decided that that town, with all those folks so loud,
Was for it a nuisance; Gur had such a large crowd,
Well secured by strong gates, well guarded night and day.

Its walls had crowning slots with horns of buffalos.
They were tall and sturdy, not one inch was hollow.
The mighty blue ocean with its relentless waves,
Would slam against these walls, potential somber grave.

Instead of black mastiffs in their kennels barking,
Two enormous dragons from the Nile caught striking,
Trained by a wise magus, watched over faithfully,
On both sides of the gate, day and night, docilely.

But one night this lion, overwhelmed by its frown,
Jumped over the sea gulch, landed before the town
And furious, tore right down with its ferocious bite,
The gate of the city, fiery dragons to smite.

He tumbled down the walls, stepped over the two beasts,
Leveled all to the ground with paws turned into fists
And when it was all done, heading back for the shore,
The proud city of Gur was but rubbles galore.

All that was left standing to recall its nature
Were some remnants of wall to respite the vultures.
This lion rested calm, yawning on its belly.
No loud roar, no roaming, pondering steadily

Over its condition, caught by those cunning men,
Its pangs did not bother. It was bored in this den.
The other three paced up and down the bony cave
If a bird would fly by the railings of their grave

They'd jumped up and just gnawed in anticipation,
  Causing a foamy surge from their salivation.

And suddenly in some corner of their prison,
The bar door flung opened. They sprang in unison.
A man was shoved inside, robed in a white tunic,
Thrown in to the lions as well-deserved picnic.

The barred gate was closed, a lugubrious sound.
There, in the somber cave, to a certain death bound,
The man met the lions, famished, angry, wrathful,
With mane ruffled, foaming, they could see the mouthful

They would make of this prey. So they rushed, roaring loud,
With that rage that ensues from pangs too long in shroud,
  And their nature of beast, fierce, wild and yet irate
  With justice for their race, captive under this grate.

So the man said: "Lions, Shalom Aleichem!"
And he rose up his hand, and put a stop to them.
The wolves chasing corpses, and dig them up often,
The bears, great flesh rippers, the jackals, too rotten

And ferocious that prey mostly when ships are down,
  Infamous hyenas cause any hunter's frown.
The patient tiger hunts, then jumps to make its kill,
  But the mighty lion, king of the jungle still,

Rarely goes for a kill then chooses to desist
Since it lords it over any created beast.
So the lions convened, in unsettling sudden,
And deliberated in the tenebrous den,

Like a group of elders debating a matter.
So they frowned their whiskers, in their royal chatter.
Life came to a standstill, tree branches froze steady,
Nature feared the issue, lurking this tragedy.

The sand lion, solemn, uttered and said: "Lions,
When this man was pushed in, through this gate of iron,
I felt like a warm gust, just like in the desert,
And I felt all over the same strength I exert

When I battle strong winds, in the heat of the land.
This man is sent to us straight from the desert strand".
The lion of the woods said: "Back in time, the concert,
Of fig trees, of palm tress, of cedars though inert,

Their branches steady flow would bring joy to my den.
Even at eventide, when all sleep, even then,
I would hear the foliage sing softly to my ears.
When I heard this man's voice, it dispelled all my fears,

Just like on tree branches, the birds sing in their nests,
This man is sent to us by the mighty forest".
The lion which first came to face up this strange man,
The one of the mountains said: "Whosoever remains

Standing straight like a rock? The Caucasus Mountains,
Where rock never troubles. That was my old domain.
When he rose up his arm, he favors the Atlas.
He resembles to me old Lebanon, --Alas! --

With mountains hovering, shedding shade in the plains.
This man, I feel strongly is sent by the mountains".
The lion of the sea, which roamed the dunes and shore,
Which roared loud as the sea, even when waves would soar,

Spoke the last and so said: "As son, it's my nature,
Each time I face greatness, my sadness takes leisure.
That's why I love the sea and its immensity.
I would gaze at the waves and their intensity.

I would watch the sunrise and the moon silver streak,
The infinite darkness would smile when the dawn peaks,
And I got, O lions, in that intimacy,
Used to eternity in all its secrecy.

But whatever the name that for him they define,
In the eyes of this man, I saw the heavens shine.
This man here, so serene, this man was sent by God.
When the night shed its veil and stars came out their pods.

The jailer peeped to see what became of that slave.
He put his face against the cold bars of the cave,
And in a dark corner, there, saw Daniel standing,
Bathing in ecstasy, Heaven contemplating,
Pondering peacefully over the starry fleet,
While the lions docile, lovingly licked his feet.

The great spin

Under the glare of the hot sun
Where life thrives down to the unknown,
Under the mantle of the sun
We all strive with tasks of our own.

The birds pick at all they can find
The flowers suck up from the soil
The beasts to beasts are not so kind,
They battle hard to get their spoil.

But Mother Earth rolls rapidly
Half of hers chores, half of hers rests.
Always with care she steadily
Night and day serves her very best.

And we all go rollercoasting
We all enjoy her subtle ride
We all night and day do our thing
Caring for the ones by our sides.

For minding the brethren's always
The most important way to go.
It sets us up upon our ways
With blessings trickling down in row.

So there in the cosmos she springs
Rotating fiercely on axis
She has many children to bring
To light and warmth that they so miss.

Relentlessly she thrusts her mass
Around this so dangerous sun
Aware of what would come to pass
At the least misstep on her run.

So she goes day and she goes night
Keeping a keen eye on the glare
That at the same time, scorching might
Can nurture and give so much care.

Folks flout the impending danger
But yet she minds their well-being.
To her prowess they're all strangers,
Taking for granted her fleeing.

She brings her seasons and her rain
Her dear multitude to amuse
And steadily sings her refrain
To all the ones she keeps enthused

She crosses epochs and eras
Never missing a rendez-vous
Carrying so many auras,
The dark ones and bright ones she coos.

In her journey throughout the years
She's never missed on her mission
To show the God who gently steers
And keeps her in track and action.

For daily she reveals His love,
Her steadiness, His faithfulness.
His divine care comes from above
That with eyes shut one can witness.

She spins rapidly like a top
Yet never misses a sunshine
At light speed through each year, no flop,
Every season she brings is fine.

She swings oceans, she swings mountains
Yet her vales are not overflown.
The sea its bed of stone retains
And the mounts they stand on their own.

She cools herself and chosen crowd
By drawing water from the sea,
By forming huge and heavy clouds
That pour deluge when fit they see.

And she feeds, craddles and nurtures
Providing for all she carries.
She has all grains in her nature
And her harvest never tarries.

The richness deep in her bosom
Could feed the multitude she reels
As mother she wants them to come
And share with all rather than steal.

And so she goes by day by night,
Offering chores and giving rest
But rest assured, she has the might
Given to her to do her best.

The glow of her sister planet
Always caresses her dark side.
She spins like a lucent hornet
But next to Earth always abides.

They run and spin and do their thing
Always aligned not to bother
Steadily they follow their swing
While never nearing the other.

And yes she has other siblings
The clear firmament shows their shape
Some much bigger, others have rings
But none has the moon at its nape.

But she keeps her trajectory
Well secured by her Creator
No other star has history
As enticing to narrators.

Though at every spin of her run
Earth remains torn from pole to pole
Her beauty the galaxy stuns
Her archangels have firm control.

Under the warmth of the bright sun
That shines for one and shines for all,
Always when Earth by God is spun
His blessings over us befall.

The Mother

And she wakes up, her night half spent,
She's up early, her dreams all bent.
She looks kindly at her offspring
The two sunshines of her dull world
The apples of her eyes, her pearls
Those causing her heart chords to ring.

She ponders over tomorrow
Bringer of fears and of sorrow.
Having herself so much endured.
How much would she give of her life
For theirs not to be so pain rife
And she prays for their bright future.

For she had gone through misery
Suffered from farthest memory
But knows so well that through it all
Though all seemed bleak, bereft of hope
The means given for her to cope
Always came from the Lord of all.

He the Master, the Creator
He from whom trickles all splendor
Lovingly carries His children
From generations since of old
Through thick or thin, through heat or cold
Never faulting their daily grain.

Therefore she prays, Her best asset.
Their lives into His hands she sets.
And as she prays so fervently
As she surrenders at His feet
All her suff'rings and their merits
Pour blessings on her family.

Your Eyes

Lakes of the bluest waves
Reflect the sky above
And the clouds come and pave
A steady trail of love
Before never heard of.

And the sunny meadows
Bearing the month of May
Seem to give the rainbow
A colorful dismay
Worthy of pure Almay.

But when I see your eyes
At each glorious dawn
My soul all mesmerized
As ingenuous a fawn
Caught in the fairest lawn

Come whisper to my heart
Still in lunar slumber
Then the stampede that starts,
Sets fires bright amber
On walls of my chamber.

Your eyes, in the exile
Land where I don't reside
Set the mood on the isles
To rekindle the tide
Where my destiny hides.

Your eyes take for a spin
My soul and make it grow
Come the thick or the thin
Into a lovely glow
Of Winter's purest snow.

My Lord

From the depths of my soul I come to thy presence
With the wheels of my mind deflated, no essence
In what I want to be to run the few errands
My conscience wide awake received right from thy Hands.

But in my frightened heart, the pump where my life flows,
I have thy Word engraved, I uphold all thy laws.
Every beat of this heart says of thy Mightiness
And every breath I take thy Name, my Lord I bless.

Ominous threat

There in the sky of somber coat
There all over, there, everywhere,
Birds are flying fast to denote
To us below, those who still care,
The reasons of this knot in throats.

But we all guessed what it could be,
We all pondered on its nature,
We all, old timers and newbies,
Wondered this time how to secure
This treasured land of Jollibee.

The moon in the sky gave its signs,
Its pallor everyone noticed.
Its soft light seems to trigger sighs
From the chests of those watching this
Impending ruin from these dark skies.

And on the lake where all swans rule,
Where the moon mirrors its kindness,
The birds seen usually so cool,
Just can't contain their nervousness.
Their instinct just cannot be fooled.

And so nightfall besets the land
Where the heartbeats are all racing.
Deep in the chests where all lives blend,
The lamps reveal in their shining
An atmosphere of pure doomland.

Night of terror, night full of dread,
Night meant for lovers to cuddle
But that now pitilessly spreads
On every lake, pond and puddle
This sense of fear, heavy as lead.

But tell me birds, you high above
You that perch high up from the soil,
You the wild ducks or you the doves,
Whose business this ordeal comes spoil,
This trickles from what side of love?

O firmament that temper throws,
O firmament of blessings rife,
O firmament that all hearts knows
And keeps them pumping of your life,
Save us from these internal throes.

But here on Earth where simmer dreams,
Where all try to make them come true,
Where we don't even bother trim
The lies from the truth that is due,
We suffer from all that it seems.

Dreams on the mind, dreams in the heart,
Dreams that lessen daily hardship,
Dreams that gladden us from the start
And keep us from counting the sheep,
Come dry all tears that you impart.

As the Earth swaps its yin for yang,
As the sun blesses other shores,
As the shadows throw silent bangs
While all minds dream and deep throats snore,
Its other side deals with its pangs.

For the darkness only covers
Humanity's crucifixion.
For all sins silently hover.
In the spiritual addition
Nothing that's due is looked over.

But the spirit all causes plead
For it sees what we'll never know
With silent tears, it stands livid
For its warnings loudly echoed,
When facing karma and its speed.

But the loud soundless threat remains
In the dark sky of everyone.
For some their sun never regains
Its shine by strong shadows outdone
And made eternal all their pain.

And all the firmament brightness,
All of the sacraments power,
All the sermons and their prowess
Their dark soul will never shower.
They cling hard to their hopelessness.

Right there above in their dark sky
With nightmares and loud snore in throats
Birds of all sizes are flying high,
To give account on bleeding notes
Of weaknesses the world swears by.

Good Old July

In this my land of broken dreams,
Where all come apart at the seams,
All out of sync, before their time,
Like children when they lost their rhyme.

Like gliding winds on frozen lakes,
Forgotten thoughts of what's at stake,
The silent casts off a sorrow
That deep in your sand you burrow.

Through thick or thin the sun will shine
As a promise of love divine.
When it delivers your blessings
At your front door is where it rings.

And always when the sky is blue
Through the trees the sun winks at you.
Over nature shades of gladness
Bring about joy in every chest.

And all alone the paths one takes
Weeds and daffodils the sun bakes
Evenly all through the hot day
Until the rain, the sky comes spray.

They bring songs to Mother Nature
All caught in daze of her rapture.
She takes all in and so shivers
In turn fragrances delivers.

Every atom of air exults
Praising God in silent tumult.
The tree with wooden poker face
All evenly receive the grace.

And so July always simmers,
Claiming the essence of summer
And though nature's in a hurry
She never misses January.

The waves repossess all the dunes
Crafted during the month of June.
They come caress, ever daring,
The shore and all its living things.

And the sea roars, fierce and mighty
Crowning each wave with foam salty,
Steadily flowing broken dreams
Come to remind of this life stream.

This state of things is so fragile
Yet glides on shore of every isle
To bring right out of every soul
The love that deep inside it holds.

Then spurs right out of every chest
A hymn or tune bound to attest
That deep within, where life lingers,
Hope evermore remains stronger.

Hand in hand, well aware or not,
The mirrors of all broken thoughts
Reflect the rebirth of the hopes
Reminding not to brood and mope.

For all is forever given,
Falling on the laps now and then,
Rolling freely from Heaven's slopes
Solely with prayer as a dope.

It's related among seasons.
The skeptic ignores the reasons
But when at his front door it knocks
He only sees a stroke of luck.

Deep inside amid of all this
I feel overcome by the bliss.
All somber thoughts washed by the sea
And I fall at the wave mercy.

I long forgot the time of day.
And whereabouts of month of May
Lay much too heavy on my mind;
So much I left the world behind.

Always, always with no warning
Your cello can play lighter strings
For under heaven's canopy
You see how stars can be floppy.

But all the while as the sun bakes,
Fixing Mother Nature's mistakes
The raging waves come and attune
All life aspects on every dune.

And so nature will never fail
Regardless of what it entails,
To bring about in due season
Blessings for all hidden reasons.

Blessèd Hope

If I still write these lines, O my dear one, they're all for you
So you'll come to me and kindle this old flame anew.
If I still jot verses, my love one, they'll speak of you,
You the soul I seek and will pursue my whole life through.

I keep deep within every single of these instants
When breathing the same air, we could shut the door to the world,
Feeling so complete for to each other so present,
Nothing we thought could come and take away our precious pearl.
There was no need for words, the exchanged glances knew so well,
Funny how love could flow straight from Heaven's blessed well.
But deep inside me stirs the hopes that my love, swell.

If I write these poems, my darling, they all speak of you,
Of you the angel I dedicate my whole life to
If I scribble again silently I plead with you
That one day you'll return and be my mistress anew.

So many attempts I made to chase you off my mind,
Painted you with darkness, when the heartaches would overwhelm,
When the air was lacking, from my missing you too blind,
When no one would compare, of my heart you had the helm.
I'd jump at the call of your name, sweetest sound to hear,
Would follow strangers, when I think you are near.
But I keep faithfully the hope that dries my tears.

If I write these stanzas where your name rings through and through
It's just to remind you that my love for you is true.
If I write these quatrains where I seem to beg of you
It's so you come back and be my loving squeeze anew.

Town Quiesence

Over the garden in the street
Catch the echo steady racket,
Either toiling, loud epithets,
Life goes on while laundry is neet

Hanging under a rusty sun,
Amid the evening aromas,
Stiffling the day and its dramas,
As a tocsin's rung by some nun.

A grinder cart timbres away,
Drowning in the day steady fuss
The soft horn of a public bus
Emerges then it treads its way.

And as the dusk colors the day,
A cloud unveils a moon quarter,
Nature again sees the barter,
The night the day upstage away.

Don't make a sound, feel the silence
Always so fleeting, so subtle,
Come closer and in love cuddle,
In this town and its quiescence.

Turgeau

Faces of early seventies,
Anchored deep in my memory,
I see your trace in a hurry
As my younger brother I tease.

Loudly the sun glides on the porch,
The shoe shiner his change awaits.
The fowl declines the rooster date
So distasteful was its approach.

And soon the old maid will depart
Well imbued of her instructions.
The different kind of provisions
Will have to fit in her old cart.

The first meal that she has prepared
Seems to have pleased every palate.
The stomach of the whole estate
For which so many years she cared.

Loudly now resonates the horn
Of this bright decorated van.
It comes always this time past ten
With those so many flags adorn'.

The four corners of that old house
Have come alive to say the least.
That young made frantically assists,
Before he boards, this youngster's blouse.

Then my mother to us reminds
That time awaits no one ever,
That minding it is thus clever
Or else this puts you in a bind.

After a long trepidant rush
The bunch will get ready to leave
For school, not before they receive
From the Spirit the silent touch.

I push open the old green gate
And shuffle lively through the crowd.
The lines of cars with horns out loud,
To move ahead are desperate.

The crowd of kids lugging book bags
Thickens with each passing minute
And forcing through your way in it
Demands skills and a vernal drag.

And the cars sing and this echo
Into the ears makes a carnage
And the large crowd holds you hostage,
Waving before the Canado.

Petty merchants are all around
Offering their variety.
Cigarettes, cookies and candies,
Any kind of snack can be found.

But lo! There, crossing the corner
With the cop directing the peak
Of this all bottleneck traffic
With flow that'd slow any "flanneu".

Now turn into the gas station
With two overwhelmed attendants,
Ignoring how it's not prudent
To smoke during their transactions.

And the kids sitting in the cars,
For the most part still half asleep
Frantically taking a last peep
At some reading undone thus far.

While in the blue car up ahead
The voice of an irate mother
Seems to the kids bring no bother
For they too have eyelids of lead.

And you walk down this busy street
Through the small crowd of the Kinder
That today seems to be kinder,
All kids are brought into their seats.

All of a sudden emerges
That noise crowning above the crowd.
It resonates, drilling so loud
Then it dies down and resurges.

This old house with the iron gate
Where that old dog chased me one day,
On the front porch where it once lay,
Offers no clue of the pooch fate.

See this great wall Evangelist
Announces the parochial school
Whose yard offers a khaki pool
Of kids in row to say the least.

And still the parents in hurry
Come disembark their progeny.
Softly you hear Serge Regiani
Amid the morn silent fury.

Everyone rush to be somewhere.
Life is brewing, percolating
And this episode recurring
Brings no change to this thoroughfare.

Drivers are vociferating
Enraged at this slow-moving string
Of cars tangled up in this sting
Of two guys street excavating.

Now this explains that noise once heard
That was so loud but yet unseen.
This is the reason why obscene
Exchanges fly amid this herd.

From afar you hear church bells ring.
It's eight o'clock in this quarter
But Au Galop did not falter
To gather in the folks' offspring.

Then as usual I leave Turgeau
And veer into CRA road.
A truck full of gravel downloads
The street to repair undergo.

Hence was of my old neck of hood
A glimpse of morning rush hour,
And such memories still devour
My heart as often as they would

For there were rooted all my hopes
And there as well sprang my crosses
That life mercilessly tosses,
Of its journey you can't elope.

Every fiber of my being,
Every stroke of acquired strength
Mastered subtly but at great length
Was hewn from this era I sing.

Boaz in slumber

Boaz came lay himself down, worn out, weary and beat;
Having spent the whole day working hard in his field,
He then set up his doss, eager the night to yield
Right next to his farmland filled with bushels of wheat.

This old man owned large fields of wheat and of barley.
Although rich that he was, he tended to justice,
Not a thought of mischief in his mind had hospice,
Not a drop of venom in the words he'd trolley.

His beard favors silver, of the purest of grey.
He carried deep inside no mean or hatred gene
When some poorer gleaner would come across his scene:
"Drop a few cobs behind, just for her", he would say.

He walked a narrow path, shunning all crooked schemes.
Robed in integrity, of the purest affect,
And always to the poor, the ones they would reject,
His sacs of golden grains for them had no esteem.

Boaz as a good master and a caring parent,
Was always generous but thrifty in affairs.
All the ladies sought him much more than the young heirs,
For the young is handsome but Boaz was eminent.

The elder emerging from the most precious well,
Nears his end of cycle, leaving the fake behind,
In the eyes of the youth a burning flame you'd find,
While in the elder's sight the true light comes to dwell.

In the thick of the night, Boaz slept among his folks.
Near the milestones silenced favoring catacombs,
The sleeping harvesters, of fatigue lie there, numb.
Twas once upon a time, that old time I evoke.

The tribes of Israel were then far from being huge.
The ground in that era, where one would sleep concerned
By the giant footprints still fresh one could discern,
Was yet wet and much soft from that mighty deluge.

So Boaz in restful sleep, reclined under the trees,
As once slept old Jacob and as once did Judith.
Then a door was open from the heavens zenith
And over his slumber a dream came put its tease.

So unfolded the dream and Boaz saw a great oak,
Soaring from his entrails straight to the sky above.
A race in long string rose, as though pulled by sheer love,
And below a king sang, Heavens a Son evoked.

Boaz in his soul murmured, lost in his confusion:
"How can this be, O God, that I beget all this?
The number of my years, you must have surely missed,
I don't have any son; have no wife, no union.

"A long time it has been since the last mate I had.
She departed O God, for your blessed azure,
Though we remain still one, love everything endures,
She still lives in my heart that now lives just a tad.

"I would beget a race! It's so hard to conceive.
How is it that just now I'd have a progeny?
As a young man flaming, sons, one can have many.
The night always repairs what the day so deceives.

"But when old ones tremble, like the birch in winter.
I am old and alone and see nearing the end.
My head, my life, my soul, toward the tomb all bend,
Like a deer to the brook, after a light sprinter."

Thus deep within his soul Boaz muttered in the dream,
As he looked up to God, in this somnolent phase.
The great oak doesn't feel the meek rose at its base,
Just like Boaz failed to see the woman at his seams.

And while he lay sleeping, there, Ruth a Moabite,
Came to rest at his feet, with breast seeking fresh air,
Expecting silently some secretive affair,
When rising from slumber Boaz would then see the light.

Boaz remained there clueless of Ruth's longing for him,
And Ruth never fathomed her meek part in God's plan.
The asphodel essence with the fresh air would blend,
And over Galgala, the night unwrapped its schemes.

The night favors union, majestic and solemn,
Invisible angels hovered as sheer witness
For in the somber sky, in blessed covertness,
You'd perceive here and there of angel wings the stem.

And Boaz sleeping rhythm, peaceful and repairing,
Mingled in its cadence with the trickling of brooks.
Nature at this season as balmy as it looks
For on every hilltop, lilies were seen blooming.

Ruth pondered, Boaz slumbered, and the shadows connived.
And the herd bells quivered in the somber shelter.
Of goodness crude and bare the air did not falter,
And lions peacefully to single brook arrived.

All in Jerimadeth as in Ur was asleep,
The somber heavens dome glittered with shiny stars.
And the soft crescent moon vamped the sky from afar
And weighing all this night, Ruth inside had to keep,

Thoughts ablaze, eyes ajar, yet awake in her sack,
What genie so skillful, master of summer breeze,
Could have possibly shed, in some fortunate tease,
Such a lovely crescent amidst the starry pack!

Desamor

When I sit and take it all in
I feel so lost while traveling
The labyrinth of all your lies,
The very cause of all my sighs

I went bright eyed and bushy tailed
On your vast sea without a sail
Putting all trust in your brown eyes,
Surfing your waves of any size.

I had put all my trust in you,
In your sea and your sky so blue,
But I was riding a mirage,
So well hidden by your visage.

Now dejected down to the soul,
Traumatized by all I was told
I shun now every talk of love
Keeping my heart in its alcove.

No love vows as they all promise,
No sweet nothings, no talks of bliss,
Whether as a joke or for real
They disrupt my peace of heart still.

For me all was so true and bright,
All my wrongs you came and made right,
So naturally rolled down my lips
Rose tenderness, warmth of tulips.

But no longer will I utter
Any sweet word in cheap chatter.
I will no longer trust in them
Since my heartache they cause to stem.

The sucker punch my heart endured
Taught me a lesson, this I'm sure.
Twas a steep price, I won't forget,
And don't perceive any reset.

So don't talk to me about love
No one will come my heart to shove.
I took it hard but grasp it well,
No one to me cheap lies will tell.

The road is long, of souls so full,
But dark ones have the sweetest pull,
They take pleasure at your demise
To them you're just a common prize.

Love bliss

Never when love blesses our shore
Has it given any warning
It lands softly within the core
And it's so thrilling.

And right there we are dumbfounded,
Right there, hung snuggly by its hook,
Right there we're gently elated
By the ease it took.

My most beautiful love song
Is sung to the love of my life,
No matter the land she grew on
She'll come settle my every strife.

It rains down its golden droplets
On hearts that pine from fondness drought,
And right there give them clear outlets
To chase sullen pouts.

It comes clearer than any dawn
To change the landscape of the face,
With gentle rays it warms their lawns,
Blots the dark holes trace.

It redirects their every step
Away from hatred darkened halls
For it only hears sounds that leapt,
Bouncing off Heavens' blissful walls.

And we see tests, proofs and all toils
As means to render it stronger,
For it grows amid all turmoil
And lasts way longer.

It takes the souls that meet down here,
Predestined to receive its bliss,
To the heavens among their peer
Whose sufferings have ceased.

To me the sweetest love of all
Is the one who will come my way,
She already has heard my call,
And one day will land, come what may.

For years will come, and years will go,
Raining down all their miseries,
But in the heart all love will grow,
Brewing reveries,

Reflecting what is deep inside,
Reflecting what the mind is fed,
Reflecting what the Spirit hides,
All by Heavens led.

And so we go through life's journey
Carried in arms of the Father.
HE gives suckers to so many
Good and bad, till the great Gather.

One day happy, and one day sad,
On this well known rollercoaster
Of this the brain can become mad,
Reading its poster.

But all the while the bliss remains,
Enthralling the young and the old.
We love the joys, suffer the pains,
Making the heart bold.

But never would have we traded
This feel any other to spouse.
Love never leaves a soul jaded,
Ever ready its world to douse.

Adoration

Give praises to the Lord, all who on earth are living,
Come all on bended knee!
In the Host let's adore the God-man, our God-Kin
With fresh incense and sweet harmony. -- Refrain

With hymns of thanksgiving and gladness
Let's praise the Lord and His Heart so clement
And for His kindness confess:
O Lord we adore You, in the Blessed Sacrament! (2)

Never fathomable is His ocean of mercy,
The Lord loves us so much!
On the altar displayed, He sheds all past secrecy
At His feast He wants us all to rush. -- Refrain

He dwells within us all, our Redeemer and Master,
So kind and so loving.
He remains forever the Victim and good Pastor,
He leads us always to His Dwelling. -- Refrain

In the manger, newborn, He comes to us as Brother,
His might and divinity shed.
On the cross, as ransom, He's the Lamb of the Father,
At the mass, He's the true living Bread. -- Refrain

Down the road

(Air of "As it was")

Deep in your eyes,
Right there so deep in your eyes,
I can see but coldness instead
But you want to cuddle in bed.

Standing confused,
Of kissing not at all enthused,
All you say I've already heard,
Your actions are drowning your words.

Ooooooh!
Here we stand, you and I,
You know we will make it down the road
Here we stand, please don't cry,
There's always someone else down the road,
Down the road
Down the road

Try to be strong
You know we'll have to go on
Many before us went that way
Really nothing left to be said.

Of all our plans
I can see that nothing remains.
It's always easy to break a heart,
Now just walk away with your part

Oooooh!
Here we stand, you and I,
You know well we'll make it down the road,
Here we stand, don't you cry
We will laugh of all this down the road,
Down the road
Down he road.

But no I won't tell,
I'll let them know you did well
They'll go all and crucify me,
Curse my assumed bigamy.

Oooooohh! Here we stand!

Love refrain

So jolly it sounds the refrain
Of this love that I sing to you.
So jolly and it's not in vain,
That I holler it through and through.

The birds in the air put a halt
To their daily frolicking chant,
The flowers silently exalt,
Their fragrances in the air spent.

The brook conveys to the willows
The cadence of its every score,
In return they bow very low,
Showing gladness right from the core.

Always with lyrical prowess
It sings of you, my sharona,
You my most blessed of mistress,
The precious part of my manna.

Of this love refrain I sing you,
The jolly air will always ring
For where there's love, there I'll see you,
Who to my heart happiness, bring.

...And Christ faced up the tomb

...And in those days Jesus, in Judea remained,
Having loosened the bond of a girl kept in chained,
Given ears to the deaf, healed the stranded lepers,
The bitter priests watched Him, plotting at the vespers.
As He was returning from healing the many,
Lazarus, his good friend, was sick in Bethany.
Mary and Martha were his sisters. So Mary,
To her loving Master, reclining all weary,
With the rarest perfume, had one day washed the feet.
Jesus loved them all so, the three, with no deceit.
Then someone came tell Him: "Lazarus expired."
But the crowd kept coming; He could not retire.

He taught about the laws, the books and the symbols,
Like Elisha and Job, used many parables.
He would say: " The kingdom of God can be likened
To a man plowing hard any given garden,
Who finds a precious pearl, well hidden in the ground.
He then goes on to sell all things that can be found
And hurriedly goes back to purchase the whole land.
I am the truth, the life and the way that God sends.
No one can come to me unless my God beckons."
He instructed them all with life giving lessons.
But He said to his friends, the ones always with Him:
"Lazarus, our dear friend, is asleep", with deep scheme,

"Let's go then wake him up." The disciples followed
With a rather large crowd of curious folks in tow.
But from Jerusalem, where the crowd kept the stalk,
Bethany was distant of a three-daylong walk.
Through the long, dusty roads He had gone many times,
Even the sun bright shine could not eclipse the prime

Of his clothing all white, as bright as eyes could see.
He walked to show them all the depths of God's mercy.
At Jesus approaching, Martha rushed to Him first,
And falling at His feet, she came in tears to burst:
"If you were here, Master, he would have never died."
Then sobbing ever more:" But in the tomb he lied.
You came too late." Jesus replied: "What do you know?
The Sower has power over all that He sows."

Mary remained inside, still stricken by sorrow.
Martha shouted to her: "Come, the Master's a show."
She came out. Jesus said: "Why are you so upset?"
Mary kneeled at His feet: "You would have never let
My brother die, Master, had you been with us here."
Jesus replied: " Mary, dry your tears, have no fear.
I am truth, life and way; happy those who uphold
The teachings I reveal and follow what I've told
For even if they die they will have life again;
All this while Didymus, called Thomas, more faith gain'.

Then the Lord standing there before John and Peter,
Said to the curious crowd following Him after:

"Where then have you put him?" They replied: "Come and see."
They pointed an old field with a few standing trees
And a river running over a stony ground,
A cave… And Jesus wept the whole crowd to dumbfound.

So out loud they exclaimed: "See how much He loved him!
He who chases Satan, they say, and ruins its schemes,
Would He, if He were God, as all over they claim,
Let perish a dear friend? This would be such a shame!"

Then Martha took Jesus and led Him to the cave.
As it's common a stone was placed over the grave.
"I trust in you O Lord, said Martha but after
Four days there is a stench, so thought John and Peter."

Said, Jesus: "O Woman, if you believe, today
You will see the glory of God in its display."

He said: "Remove the stone!" Right away this was done.
You could see in the tomb, as the large stone was gone.

And the Lord walked alone, leaving behind the crowd,
With eyes to His Father, towards the corpse in shroud,
   As to some sure treasure buried from the curious;
Bending towards the dark, called out loud: "Lazarus!"

Right then the dead walked out, alive and staggering
From still being tied up hands and feet with strong strings.
   He stood leaning against the wall of the deep cave.
Jesus said: "Free this man!" You could hear the crowd rave,
   And they believed in Him, Jesus, the God sent Christ,
     But the priests, silently, from hatred took advice.

They gathered there in Rome and still stunned they connived,
   Knowing well that the Lord brought Lazarus alive.
Having seen the tomb burst, heard the crowd joyous screams,
   They decided therefore: "It's time now to kill Him."

After the battle

My father, this hero, with the sweetest of smile,
Trailed by this one hussar he favored from the pile
For his great bravado and his majestic height,
Made round on his palfrey, a battleground, one night.

The ground paved with corpses, as the dusk spreads its veil,
He overheard a moan, from the shadow, exhaled,
Twas a Spaniard soldier of the routing army,
Dragging his bleeding self on the road so gloomy,

Broken, groaning, livid, to everyone, half dead,
Grumbling, all weak: " Water, please, some water", with stead.
My father affected, to his favorite hussar,
Handed, from his saddle, the rum of his small jar,

Saying: "Here, give a drink to this dying poor soul."
But as the hussar bent to his back grab a hold,
The man, kind of Moorish, his gun held in hand still,
Aiming at my father, blasted his last refill.

The "Caramba" shouted came louder than the blast.
The bullet went so close; all this went by so fast,
That my father's hat flew, his startled horse jumped back.
"Give him the drink still," said Father taken aback.

The frog

What do we really know of what really matters?
The eventide falling, the tired clouds, scatters,
And on that end of day branded of thunderous rain,
Changing passing showers to tone of rusty stain,

Near a water filled rut, on the edge of this pool,
Stood a frog, all dazzled and of inner thoughts full.

(Why so much suffering and so much homeliness?
But the Augustulus, in this world, bring pure mess,
Like the worst felonies, the vilest of pustules,
So are meadow flowers, stars of sky vestibules.)

The foliage was ablaze in trees crimson painted,
The water on the grass sparkled the ground dented,

The dusk was spreading veil over Mother Nature,
All the tree birds tune down in the somber azure,
The whole world was appeased; the frog, in oversight,
Calm, shameless and peaceful, devoid of any fright,

Admired of the sky the aureole renown.
Maybe the amphibian, though curséd felt endowed,
Not a beast that has not dwelt on heavens reflect,
A despicable sloe, too vile not to inspect

The bright lightning above, shining gentle or fierce,
Not a puny monster, whose foul sight was not pierced,
By the immensity of the stars, one clear night.
A man came walking by and saw the loathsome sight

And shuddering deeply, stepped firmly on its head.
Twas a priest with a book, using his heavy tread.
A woman went about, a flower on her chest,
With her umbrella sharp, poked its eye with one geste.

And it was an old priest, and the lady, lovely.
Four schoolboys came walk by, serene, peppy, lively,
As jolly and as cruel as young schoolboys can be.
For every human being and his soul in slavery

Can relate to the plight of his early childhood.
One has the games, the thrill and springtime pleasant mood,
One has mother nearby, and stays happy always,
Being kids, running free, nothing clutters their ways,

Breathing the air, cherished, no worry, no burden,
So why not go torture a poor animal then?
The wounded frog sniveled down the small rocky trail,
At that time when the dusk in the sky spreads its veil,

The frog hoped for the night but the kids spotted him
And shouted: "Let us kill this creature!" With wild screams,
"And since it's so ugly let's torture it before."
There, laughing joyfully, children kill when they're bored,

They proceeded poking the eye of the creature
With a sharp stick of wood, cruel treatment to endure,
Right through the gaping hole of its eye still bleeding
And passersby approved seeing more blood gushing.

The fallen dusk shadowed and nurtured the dark scene
Of the frog tormented just for being obscene.
But it tried to escape, it had one leg severed
But they kept on hitting, over it they hovered,

And every blow sustained made foam the outcast
That remains thus accursed even when the sun lasts.
And the children shouted: "Is it dead? No it moves."
Still bleeding, still jolting, eye dangling, the reproved

Kept dragging through bramble and the dirt its dreadful
And bleeding, limping self, pitiful yet frightful,
Looking as though escaped from some nefarious snare.
It survived woefully all the blows, cuts and tears.

What a vile performance! What a most sordid act!
To fill up with horror what deformity lacks!
Wounded and dismembered, it went from rocks to stones,
Still breathing and bleeding, aimless and all alone,

It crawled, as if from death even it would be scorned
For being too dreadful, from this cruel treatment torn.
The kids tried to catch it by using a shoelace
But it managed to slide, through some rut from their chase.

Still bleeding it dove in, head opened, broken down,
In the soothing coolness though unafraid to drown
In the greenish cesspool, hoping to find a truce.
Could the mire ever wash this human abuse?

And the boys of springtime, elated and chatty,
Never had so much fun, all charming yet snotty.
They all yapped together, the older ones would say:
"Come here! Hey Adolph say, has it gone pass your way?

"Let's look for a big stone to finish up with it!"
And they all there gathered, hovering the small pit
Where the desperate creature yet suffered their cruel stare,
Ecstatic in their fun, furious in what they dared.

-Hélas! We're aim loaded but remain target free!
Aiming at any point of the large human tree
Be it with life in mind and not with thoughts of death. -
All eyes peered at the fog in the vase with no depth.

One of them carried back, a large piece of cobble,
Heavy but for evil he'd shoulder the double
Saying: "Let's see right now how this is gonna end."
But right at this instant, on this same spot of land,

Came around a carriage, heavy as full of lead,
Pulled by an old donkey, meager, deaf, with no stead.
The ass all exhausted, crippled and pitiful,
After a long day walk, its barn was near to pull.

It dragged the big carriage and carried loads as well,
For each step you could see, the next, could not foretell.
The beast moved by the whip, worn out and livid,
The whips rained all over, forceful, mean and rapid.

In its eyes you could see a vague and cloudy stare
Made of dullness that seemed to be devoid of care,
With orbits deep sunken and filled with crusty mud,
With its side so hard that each spin made a dull thud.

And the ass kept whining and the owner, swearing,
The road had a down slope but no solace could bring
And it went on thinking, passive under the whip,
Deep where the mind of men could not possibly sweep.

The boys hearing it come, the wheel and steps as well,
Looked back, loudly yapping, saw the ass and its bell:
"Don't put the stone on it, here comes a large carriage.
Stop, stop, they yelled. There it comes down the somber ridge,"

"It will run over it, that's much, so much better."
They all looked. Suddenly, amongst all this jitter,
Expecting the last draw for the monstrous creature,
The ass saw the poor frog and sadly, knew for sure,

To one less fortunate, - beaten, broken and torn -
It sniffed it as it seemed, lowered its head though scorned,
And managed in its woe to find a way to spare:
So pulling all its strength and stiffening the snares

Tearing up his muscles and causing them to bleed,
Ignoring its owner beating it for more speed:
"Move on!" It took control of this load much bearing,
With all its weariness jumped right into the ring,

Pulling hard the carriage and lifting up the pack,
All haggard, it shifted the wheel from its first track,
Giving the frog the chance at its miserable fate.
Then under roughest whips, headed for the estate.

Losing grip of the stone that suddenly he dropped,
One of the boys, - the one of this story the prop –
From the infinite dome, as crimson as it should,
He heard a voice utter, saying to him:" Be good!"

Clemency of dullard! Shiny pearl form the coal!
Most blessed enigma! Bright light of darkest hole!
Blessèd ones in nothing would surpass the fallen
If the latter, though lame and forever sullen,

Show pity. O beauty! Shadows lifting darkness!
The true dejected soul helping the one lifeless,
The moved dullard soothing the hideous one torment,
The gentle reprobate thrilling the one present!

The animal growing whereas the man recedes!
In the sheer quiescence, which the fallen dusk feeds
The beast at times ponders, chooses to sympathize,
Seeing subtle mildness being wrongly chastised.

All it takes is a spark of blesséd gentleness
To bring the animal to act in pure kindness.
The donkey coming home, overloaded, weary,
Exhausted to the bones, muscles sore, all dreary

Musters strength for more steps, executed in pain,
Not to crush a poor frog, though it might be in vain.
This despicable dunce, soiled, bruised under the whip,
Wiser than Socrates, over Plato, took leap.

So you ponder, wise man, and you poet, meditate?
You're seeking for the truth on this land desolate?
Take deep in and treasure love unfathomable!
The true light of this world, rare yet attainable,

The true light of this world, that makes an ass, angel.
Love that depicts this world and its darkness, dispels,
Love in shape of a dawn with golden drops of dew,
Love that soothes human hearts into ticker brand new,

Impulse felt in the dark, amid deep misery,
Is the deep hidden link, divine and plenary,
That connects much subtly, hélas! So mystically,
The donkey, stupid beast to God, the Almighty.

The bed we no more share

This lonely bed ladden
Of treasured souvenirs
Upon which you lay then
When toward you I'd steer,
That yet keeps so concealed
The stormy escapades,
The times I'd make appeal
When you suffered mood trade,
Offers a silent stare,
This bed we no more share.

This relic that remains
Witness of our debates
That often put a strain
On our romantic state,
Remembers the long nights
You stayed awake wondering,
Concerned by all the fights
That our bond were tearing,
Keeps all with no fanfare
This bed we no more share.

In condolence with all my pain
Watches me reach for you in vain,
And of this love tearing me wide apart
Wonders will it one day from me depart?

This bed of me and you
That now misses you blind
That sends muttered boohoo
To strangers that it finds,
Trespassing on your turf,
This spot I hold so dear
And that it keeps reserved,
That's to my heart so near,
Feels like: how can I dare,
On it we no more share.
This oh so lonely bed
Will span through life right here,

This life heavy as lead
That your mere absence sears,
This bed would give its life
To wrap you in its sheets,
Satin caress' so rife
All to a queen so fit,
Hold you in loving snares,
This bed we no more share.

This wooden bed so strong
Soothes all my aches away,
Sorting where they belong
The weary thoughts I lay,

Faithfully, patiently,
Humble deep in the core,
It longs for silently
For you, dreams of encore,
This bed of solitaire
That now we no more share.

Star of life

I held so many hands, so many walked my way,
Kept many in my arms, others just ran away,
So many ones I begged, so many who forgot
Even my very name or the good side I got.

I made all promises that away have faded,
I had my share of flings that left me so jaded,
I believed in a few, was mislead by others,
While many to my croon would not even bother,

But all the while my dear, all those so many whiles,
I dreamt of you my love, of you my shiny star,
There was always something of you that, all beguiled,
Compelled me to press on but you remained afar.

There were times I regret and others I retained,
Quick instants of pleasure, and moments that now stain,
Times so clear I could swear that it was the right thing,
And the so many times of careful regrouping.

Now that gone are the days of hormonal parade,
Of mirage following and of clever charades,
I still deep in my mind entertain some prospects,
But in the midst of all, each time I introspect

It is you that I see my blessed guiding light,
You who gives to my life a clear trail to follow,
You who keep me going even in my dark night,
You I've been dreaming of, as I journey solo.

Lustation

Whenever I'm given somebody nice and kind,
There is always a witch in the back of my mind.
There, in the dark alleys of my untamed desire
She paces restlessly and ignites my fire.

Seems though I'm not aiming at anyone's offense,
The grass is just greener the other side of fence.
And for every blessing the Lord on us bestows,
The devil always tries to spoil our tomorrow.

Fierceness

If you could see through me, my dear,
You'd jump so high, you'd brag so loud,
You'd stay awake at night from fear
Of losing me, feeling so proud.

If you could see through me, my love,
You'd pray all day, you'd pray all night,
Giving thanks to the God above
For a treasure of such a might.

I remain the captive that will never escape,
The one caught in you cage of bars of purest gold,
The one who willingly fixes every known gape,
The one who would not leave based on what was foretold.

If you could see through me, I say,
There would be stars in your blue sky,
There'd be warmth in your winter days,
And birds would sing when you'd go by.

If you could see through me you'd see
The fierceness of my love for you,
Strong enough to cross any sea,
Strong to make all your dreams come true.

Someone like you

The first time I saw her face
I fell right into her trace.
It is not every Sunday
That suddenly comes your way
Someone like you.

She was jolly, and peppy,
Making her whole world happy,
On that lovely autumn day,
She went rolling on the hay,
As you would do.

So I asked her for her name,
What country she gives such fame,
She giggled then looked at me,
Weighing my anatomy
Like angels do.

For a while I felt impelled
Standing there under her spell,
To ask if she'd ever met
Anyone just like her set,
Someone like you.

Instead we chatted along,
Had to find ways to prolong
This encounter so bizarre,
Unprecedented thus far
With one like you.

I poured my heart easily,
Almost like making a plea.
She took all with empathy,
As though my life was worthy
Of one like you.

Of herself revealed nothing,
As if she had no meaning,
Willfully took the back seat
Just like had done in repeat
Someone like you

Then she explained earnestly
Like a muttered homily
That patience was a virtue
Regarded in highest view
By those like you,

That I should never desist
Keeping my mind on the piste
Of my heart where God reveals
The goodness that us here, fills,
All our lives through.

For often my hope wavers,
Its light gets feeble, quivers,
And I slip in some despair,
Aiming at other affair,
That wouldn't be you,

Human beset with weakness,
We often shape our own mess,
Trusting in any mirage
Bound to be some cheap potage,
Not one like you.

So we devise some quick plan
That we know well will not stand,
But the surging of the drive
Incites our miserable live
To then miss you.

All over were autumn leaves,
Tossed around as nature breathed.
They brought about steadily
Caresses unevenly,
Right 'pon us two.

The breeze blew a bit nippy,
But this floral entropy
Marveled my indigent soul,
Of my words I took control,
Still naming you.

And she did what she does best,
Remained silent for the rest,
As wanting to hear it all,
As sparing me from this fall
Deep into you.

Twice I offered her my coat,
Twice she rejected the quote.
She seemed to enjoy the breeze
That now was rocking the trees,
So unlike you.

Twas a Thursday, I recall,
One most precious day of fall,
And the air with drops of dew
Tickles with a scent brand new
All the way through.

The lawn under its blanket
Missed the sun that came to set,
Therefore the lake took it all,
Got gilded by nature call,
Blinding us two.

And the day ended softly
I had said all eagerly
Now the silence around us
Felt strange, made me curious.
I thought of you.

I took it she was thinking
Understood that was her thing
Not realizing that meanwhile
She let me stew in the pile
Said about you.

What she said to me after
Caused no sorrow nor laughter.
It came blunt but softly said
Over my mind made its raid,
Ceased thoughts of you.

There I remain all haggard
Because now she held the cards.
She had just kindly silenced
My mind of your love so tensed
By tales of you.

And so we walked hastily
This park was cold suddenly
To the street where leaves still flew
Carrying in sheer snafu
All that was you.

She had ransomed my psyche
Of this bind much to freaky
That lasted a small epoc
And left my heart in a shock
Pining for you.

Frankly Speaking

I will never pursue, nor envy, nor covet
In any circomstance anyone else's pet.
The yearning of the flesh becomes a great offense
For anything greener on any side of fence.

So I'll remain faithful to my basic concept,
Not eager to create any spiritual debt.
If loving to the soul is the most soothing balm,
The craving for others' is the worst of napalm.

And Then There were None

How many a young men, how many young fathers
Who left ever eager to fight the enemy,
Lulled by selected words of skillful recruiters
To fall right in the midst of this world infamy.

They were trained for the most to face all kinds of war,
Were prepared to affront fiercest adversaries
But one important piece is still missing so far,
A motive that would come to quell their inquiries.

For what was the reason to shed so precious blood,
What would be the profit of such a sacrifice?
What would change the karma of this land that they trod,
Why despite history we fell in this trap twice?

So many mums and dads, so many wives and kids,
Left without their children or still missing their spouse.
Some with help of a friend, others, from fear, livid,
Alone wishing, praying that they're back to the house.

Just a few years ago they were playing the same
On a Nintendo screen, practicing day and night.
But now the threat is real, it's no longer a game,
They're killing human beings or they feeling the fright.

So far no end in sight, so far there's no way out.
The plans are washed out, no one saw this coming.
What was so cut and dry, so carefully laid out
Is now a sheer chaos with death daily roaming.

So many ways the world tried to prevent this hell,
So many times they were reminded not to go.
So many times because of news you cannot tell
The country silently suffered this heavy blow.

And the rest of the world, in favor or appalled,
Witness' the biggest mess known to this century.
And down in history it will be justly called
The start of the downfall of this blesséd country.

How many body bags, how many heads will roll
In this modern version of Apocalypto?
How many families will have to pay this toll?
On both sides of this war their painful tears echo.

Surely all our heroes daily stumble and fall
Under the grinding teeth of that beast to be fed
But woe to whoever would have started it all,
Better it would've been not to have been born instead.

For the shedding of blood of any God's creature
Under any banner that fits your agenda,
In return will demand the adequate measures
To clean the heavy stain painted on your aura.

I salute the many, for the most part unknown,
Forced into this carnage from fear of reprisal.
The ones who enlisted hoping to find their own
Glimpse of some distant dream that turned to be fatal.

To the many mothers still clinching their sorrow,
Dreading to hear one day the ringing of the phone,
May the Master of Love , your loved ones tomorrow,
Bring to you home safely, lest one day there'd be none.

Blesséd day

Oh blesséd be that day,
That day you crossed my path!
I can honestly say
I'm glad you're in my life.

The birds on my window
When they cuddle and coo
Say there's no more sorrow
For in my life there's you.

Faith Hope Love

He who believes, Father, tends also to give love.
Remember Lord, that love begets unfaltering hope.
This is the sole reason, alone in my alcove,
I kneel down before You to meditate and mope.

You are the Creator of every entity.
With Your breath You gave life to the whole galaxy.
This world should before You, in sheer humility,
Bow the head, bend the knee and beg for Your mercy.

I hope You cast upon Your servant's misery
And total submission some of Your clemency.
You alone, my dear God, can make my life anew
And from my emptiness show the world Your virtue.

Father how I adore Your divine tenderness.
You set this spark of love so deep within my heart
That every beat it strikes is only to witness
My love for You and from Your Face never depart.

To my sister, Jacotte

Belated Reproach

You could have chosen to live much longer
We had yet so much of feelings to share,
We had yet so much, being such a pair,
Of cozy late nights with good talk over.

You could have chosen to live much longer
But you chose instead as good pioneer,
To blaze other trails, to feel other fears,
When the inquiries became much stronger.

But you could have lived like the rest of us.
Carry little aches, bearing the crosses
That come to us from the Boss of bosses
And instill in us a much deeper trust.

You could have remained with no shady doubt
And we could have gone as we so long planned
To the old country care for the orphaned,
Bring about their smiles and erase their pouts.

You could have chosen to hang out longer
But then decided no more to be pair,
Leaving me the charge to pay just one fare
When will come my time to fly thereafter.

You could have chosen to be here with us
And not to force me to write down this song,
Knowing much too well how I can prolong
The many capers with old Morpheus.

Saint John's Gospel

In the beginning was the Word
And the Word gladly was with God
And the Word, He, himself, was God!
And all things came to be through Him,
For nothing was made without Him.

What came to be through Him was life,
That life, Light of the human race,
That Light that shines in the dark strife,
That darkness just could not efface.

A man named John was sent from God.
He came to give testimony,
To testify so that many
Believe through Him in this great Light.
He was far from being the Light
But came only to testify
That the Light, source of every Life,
Into the world was due to come.

For the Light was into the world
And the world came to be through Him
But the world never knew of Him.

He came humbly amongst His own
But sadly, His Word, they disowned.
But to those who did accept Him
He gave power to be His kin,
Those who believe in His great Name,
Not born by flimsy human choice,
Nor by natural generation,
Nor by sole human decision
But only by the Will of God!

✝

And the divine Word was made flesh
And amongst us He chose to dwell!
And all eyes witnessed His glory.
His glory as of the Father's Son,
So full of Grace, so full of Truth!

John testified to Him and cried out saying:
"This is the One of whom I firmly attested
That though following me, He ranks ahead of me
Because He existed at all times, before me."

From His fullness we all received grace after grace.
The law was from Moses but through Jesus alone,
From His Father's mercy, we received Grace and Truth.
No one has ever seen the mighty Face of God.
The only Son of God, who's at the Father's side,
To the true believer, chooses to reveal Him.

Immaculate Mary

All you faithful brethren come and let's admire
The Virgen now Mother, the daughter of David…
Come all, let's admire, clothed in white attire,
A wonder in herself, utmost creation bid.

She easily conceived with the help of no man,
Purest soul mesmerized by God's wonderful deeds.
Everyday her Spirit in deep prayers remain'
She rejoiced in her soul over all that God did:
She remains a virgin, with the most treasured Child.

She, the sweetest of doves, carries the strong Eagle,
The Ancient one, snow white, his praise loudly singing:
"My Son, You the richest, chose to come and mingle
In a wretched manger. You, the melodious String,

You remained all quiet, like a child so feeble,
Allow me, if you please, that for You, my voice rings."

"Your kingdom, O my Child, surpasses all others,
But You chose my poor womb as Your precious abode.
The heavens, Your glory, could not ever smother,
But You chose the meekest to make Your divine pod."

"Allow that Ezekiel come see You on my lap,
So he can recognize the One on the chariot
Carried by cherubims …, today, You, my arms wrap.
And in a great tremor, sing in blessed riot:
Blessed be the splendor of the Place where You dwell!
But now You dwell in me, my womb is Your abode,
The throne of Your great might, in my arms, softly held."

"Come see me, Isaiah, come see and let's rejoice,
See, now that I conceived although a virgin still,
Prophet of the Spirit, with visions of best choice,
Behold Emmanuel whom you could only feel…"

"So come all you faithful, driven by the Spirit,
You who deep in your heart feel the warmth of his Love…
Stand up; give praise out loud, on bended knees, come meet,
Held gently in my arms, is the Bread from above."

Let Christmas be merry

Let there be a merry Christmas
Despite the turmoil in our world!
Let there be a merry Christmas
With warm manger and golden pearls.

Let there be a merry Christmas,
This marvel beyond all telling
That the good Lord from ages past
Sent all His prophet heralding.

Let there be a merry Christmas,
For deep within our infancy
This Gift bestowed was meant to last
Throughout our life, from God's mercy.

Let there be a merry Christmas
For God almighty chose to wear
Just for our sake a form that pass'
So, to be His children, we'd dare.

Let there be a merry Christmas,
There'll never be another one.
Beware that the next time He pass'
Of His graces you'd come undone.

For the next time He comes around
He will not be small, shivering.
With His army and blasting sound
He'll come for some serious sieving.

Let there be a merry Christmas
And make it last the whole year through
So that next time the trumpet blasts
You'd be given a life brand new.

Dreadful Way Home

Varied are the channels, the Lord in his wisdom,
Remind His children of the way to His kingdom.
For neither the hour, the time, nor circomstance
Can we know when to make before God our entrance.

On any given day, if they see the sunrise,
Great many among us face up with some surprise.
It's never expected and can be unpleasant
For never departure has been known to enchant.

So this early morning, with a light overcast,
All went on as usual around him. Not a blast.
Light breakfast, shower, shave then up to work he went,
And all he could think of was how to make the rent.

See, business had been slow. No help came from the rain
Which chose to fall so much backing up the main drain.
People had to stay home, it was more than a choice
From fear of getting soaked, fall sick and lose their voice.

This early spring has been a tad too wet for him,
It was way too early for May flower to gleam.
He deemed it was senseless for nature to downpour
So much water to change the Earth face and contour.

He walked to the kiosk, got the news he prefers,
Saw the headlines and said: "Oh wow! I so differ"!
And then he shook his head, headed for the subway,
Part of this long routine leading to work each day.

He met the neighbor's wife. They then chatted briefly.
She stopped at the cleaners, they parted there vaguely.
The sun peeped a short while, twas not gusting today,
Yesterday was a mess, the winds on us all preyed.

He went with peppy steps crossing the street corners,
Waving at passersby, familiar store owners,
Nothing seems unusual as he stepped in to buy
Black coffee and bagel at the deli Bed-Stuy.

With the deli owner after exchanging jokes,
He stepped back in the street, set for the daily pokes
A subway rider gets from other commuters.
Nothing to gripe about, just keep tight your shutters.

As he reached the stairway a crowd was exiting.
So he stood patiently but was shoved, weirdest thing,
By some guy in some rush, or some much heated chase,
The hot coffee he held spilled on pants and briefcase.

So there he stood half wet with onlookers around
Who like everybody were all rushing work bound.
Funny how small hazards can come as forewarning,
As we go on living and their message shunning!

As he stood, came roaring the train uptown express,
Feeling wet, cold, wishing he could somehow undress,
Lost in the crowd, thoughts on his now wet and cold slacks,
There came the fatal shove. He felt down in the tracks.

The destitutes

I

It's midnight. The cabin is poor but safely shut.
The abode is obscure but deep inside this hut
Something hovers subtly in this silent nightfall,
Fisherman nests dangle here and there on the walls.

There, in the corner, shines, on a bahut of oak,
Some modest tableware that better days, evoke.
You perceive a large bed with its large, drawn curtains.
Closer, an old mattress, on some benches, remains.

Five young children asleep rest on it peacefully.
In the dark standing hearth where some flames burn lively,
A reddened glow is shed. Kneeled face down on the bed,
A woman prays, ponders about the days ahead.

She is a lonely mother. And outside, the sea,
To the sky and the winds, the rocks, and mist you see,
Repeats its gloomy call, dark and lugubrious.
The man is on the sea, sailor notorious,

Who deals with dark perils under rough conditions.
Against all odds he must put aside emotions,
The kids have to be fed. He leaves then late at night
When the tide rises up and the boat dangles light.

He manages alone the boat and its four sails
While the wife left at home sowing garments she sales,
Mending nets, re-meshing, setting up the fishhooks,
Watching over the hearth, seeing the fish soup cook,

Then praying to her God after her children sleep.
All alone in the night, against all odds, he keeps
His sail straight and afloat towards the needed catch.
Hardest work! All is dark; all is cold, dreary watch,

Against reef and the sea and its tumultuous swings,
The best spot to cast nests and a good harvest bring.

But on waters so dark, so fickle and flighty,
Where swim all living things set by the Almighty,

One spot is favorable as wide as two bedrooms.
December night, misty, wavy and full of gloom,

Finding this exact spot, in this moving desert,
How difficult for one, such a spot to assert!

What careful maneuvers to rightly execute!
The waters all around slither, glide and refute.
The abyss growls within its measureless bottom,
Rattling tackles on board in moans loud and gruesome.

He misses his Jeannie along these icy seas,
And she sobs out his name and in thought secrecy,
They meet in the cold night, sweet pair of lonely birds.

She prays but the hoarse cries, mocking of birds are heard,
Troubling the gentle peace within her private world
Made of pile of rubble, the ocean, the dreadful
And all sorts of shadow keeping her so thoughtful:

The sea and its fury, taking boat and sailors,
And deep within her girth, like in trees, sap galore,
The ticking of the clock sustains the mysterious,
Drop by drop time rolls in, steady, meticulous.

And every beat pounding from the huge universe
Brings to the living soul worlds of cradles and hearse'

Gentle to foster life or harsh to seal your tomb.
And she ponders and dreams; but poverty entombs.

Her kids are barefooted and this all through the year,
No bread of wheat ever, only barley bread here.
O God! The windblasts shake the walls of the meek shack
The seashore knocks as though a yard of lumberjack.

The stars of firmament seem to have quickly flown,
Like sparkles in whirlwind over fire are blown.
That's the time of the night where, flighty and jolly,
The darkness spreads shadows, roots of subtle follies.

They come with their blindfolds to shed their sad gaiety.
They connive, rain and gloom, in deep obscurity
And then the poor sailor, shivering in the dark
Suddenly sees a rock and goes crash with his bark.

How awful! The sailor, silenced by the waters,
Feels the boat slowly sink. Oh painful disaster!
The dark abyss swallows the sailor and what flash
Are scenes of sunny shores that the sea comes to wash.

These dreary, dark visions, as scary as the night,
Shed trouble and disturb, so she trembles of fright.

O unfortunate wives of the many sailors!
O poor souls left hanging, shivering in pallor:
"Father, lover, brother, son, all I so cherished,
Fallen in this abyss! -- All I hold dear perished!"

Falling in the deep sea is to be prey to beasts.
When we think that the sea with all has silent feasts
From the smallest of foam to the dear husband boss,
And that the wind blowing haphazardly comes toss

Them hither or tither, spreading gut-wrenching stress,
And that they might also be somewhere in distress,
And that we'll never know their whereabouts at all,
That in this rolling sea so hopelessly they fall,

To all these somber gulfs, deep in which shines no star,
They just hang to wreckage to stay afloat thus far!
Gloomy thought! But we run, searching the rocky coast
But when the waters rise, never return their hosts.

Hélas! What can the sea reply to perturbed minds,
When she remains somber and raging as can find!
But Jeannie is so sad knowing her man's alone!
Alone in this rough night, under this veil dark tone!

No help! His kids are young. But you think, --O mother!
God, if they were older! They could help their father.
But later when of age, able to sail and strong,
Lost in tears you would wish that they would still be young!

So she takes her lantern and her cape for it's time
To check on his return, if he's gotten his prime,
If it's dawned, if the sea has gained some countenance,
If she can spot the light, signal of his advance.

Come on! And so she steps right out in the fresh air.
Nothing, she sees nothing. Not a line, not a glare,
Just the somber expanse where sea and sky embrace.
And it rains and the rain carries the dark sky trace.

It's as though the dawn fears to point out today
And that the day trembles at passing its doorway.
So she heads on. No light. Not a soul is awake.
Her eyes scope the darkness though worn out by her wake.

She guesses the small trail but then she sees the hut,
Decrepit and somber, as if from this world cut.
Its door by winds rattling, molded by rain and dew,
With a shaky rooftop that has long paid its dues,

Of hideous stubbles, rotten, loose and putrid.
And she thought:" This lady, poor soul and unmarried,
My husband found her sick and all by her lonesome,
Let's see if she's ok; her shack looks so gruesome."

So she knocks at the door and waits but no answer.
It is cold, she shivers, pulls her cape much closer.
"Being sick! And the kids! They look so underfed.
They are just two but she is so poor and unwed."

She knocks again. "Neighbor!" She calls out in the dark.
But dead silence resounds. "O my Lord! She remarks
She must be dead asleep and so hard to wake up!"
But the door on its hinge, as eager to make up,

For this show of pity, swung open wide slowly
She stepped in and shed light on the floor nervously
A dark, shabby cabin, devoid of least welfare,
Near the tumultuous sea, roof leaky, walls so bare.

Down there, in the darkness, was a harrowing scene.
A body on its back, barefooted, so demeaned.
A cadaver. - She could, in her past, all tackle. -
Now she lay there lifeless; poverty pinnacle.

This is then what ensues the life of the bereft.
One lying disheveled on a pallet bed, left
All alone to meet death. Her mottled arm hanging
And her hand discolored. Sight much disconcerting!

It's as if from her mouth a silent cry of fright
Would emerge right after her soul rose to its light.
This cry only perceived down in death dark valley
Whose echoes roam faintly eternity's alleys.

Near the bed where would lie the departed widow,
Two toddlers, boy and girl, in a cradle set low,
Were sleeping peacefully, smiling through pleasant dreams.
The mother sensing death approaching, as it seemed,

Put her shawl over them, along with a thick robe.
She attempted to warm, when her heart stop to throb,
Their little frail bodies from the cold that entails
The departing of soul when its time comes to sail.

See how they're both sleeping in this shaky cradle!
They breathe so peacefully. Their faces naught straddles
Nor would come to disturb these orphans in their rest,
Not even the blasting of last judgment tempest

For being innocent their meek soul are at ease.
And the steady downpour their stillness does not seize.
From the leaks from the roof drenching the mudded floor,
Still on the corps forehead, one drips in slow encore

Then rolls down her cold cheek, mimicking drops of tears.
The waves sound like the bell of an alarm in gear.
The defunct seems to heed the hovering shadows.
The body left alone after the spirit's flow

Seems to still search the life, begging her to return.
The keen eye can perceive this deep post mortem yearn,
Cold exchange of unwords, tween the mouth and dead stare:
"What happened to your breath? – And of you, where's the glare?"

Hélàs! Love, enjoy life, gather its primroses,
Dance, laugh and be merry, trip on overdoses.
Just like to the ocean runs down every river,
Fate dictates steady goal to cradles, and severs

Mother from treasured child, with merciless outcome,
To love pleasures the soul always begs to ransom,
To the songs, the laughter, to love frank, free of gloom,
Down to stunning coldness of the stone of the tomb!

So what did Jeannie do in this poor defunct hut?
Under her large capote, what is it that she brought?
What is it she carries down the trail, in the rain?
Why is her heart throbbing down this gloomy terrain?

Rushing so feverishly? Why in this dark alley
She runs with no concern, without keeping tallies?
What is it she's hiding while looking so distraught,
In the dark, on her bed? What is it that she caught?

When she rejoined her kids, a dull day was dawning.
She sat down by the bed, worn out and still gasping,
Pale and taking all in. Seeing what she had done
She worried much deeply, and inside felt undone.

Between heavy breathing, from her mouth, words in bits
Would erupt competing with the sea waves in fits.
"My poor man! Ah! My God! What will he say? He's got
So much yet on his plate! Why go increase his lot?

Five children in his care! This hard working father!
As if this was not much, I had to go farther
And bring more work for him. — Is that he? No, nothing.
I did wrong. What if he gets upset, goes screaming?

Then I'd say: You are right! — Is it he? - No. — Better.
The door moves from the wind. — But no! — Not him, later.
How I dread see him come back home now! Who would say?
Then she went on weighing the bind, in which she lay,

Shivering, taking in deep in somber anguish,
Lost in this dark torment where candid souls perish,
Lost in her troubled world, having shut everything,
The noisy cormorants, in their fight, disturbing,

And the waters roaring and the winds in fury.
And the door swung open, this time loud and hurried
Shedding down on the floor a ray of pale brightness
And the sailor dragging his sole mean of business,

Happily showed his face and said: "Tis the marine!"
"It is you, yelled Jeannie! Her bosom, deep within,
She received her husband as you do a lover
And in her warm embrace she kissed him all over
While the man kept saying: "It is I, my lady!"
Showing his face glowing from the hearth all ruddy,

His heart kind and cheerful whose Jeannie was the cause.
"I am all done, he said; a night unlike all those.
How was it there? – Vicious. – And fishing? – A big waste.
But now I'm in your arms and my sadness you've chased."

"I caught nothing at all, and even tore the net.
Tonight something evil deep in the winds was set.
What a night! I once thought, amid all this uproar,
That we would sink for sure when the boat got unmoored."

"But what did you concoct, by yourself, in that while?"
Jeannie shivered subtly in the dark but then smiled:
"I? She said. Ah! You know. Not a thing as usual.
I repaired nets", trying to sound and look casual.

"I was concerned hearing the sea in its fury.
Winter is treacherous, and it got so scary."
And shaking like a child who got caught for she lied
She said: "Oh by the way, our next door neighbor died."

"That must be yesterday she expired, but again
Maybe last night after you left, under the rain.
She leaves a pair of tads, two very young children,
The boy's name is William, the girl's is Madeleine."

"The boy's still a baby, the girl can barely talk,
The poor lady struggled deprived of the least frock."
The man pondered heavy, and throwing his bonnet
Down in the room corner, heavy, all soaked and wet:

"Goddamn it! He exclaimed, scratching frankly his head,
We have five of kids of ours, now seven to be fed.
We can barely survive during the rough season
But now what will we do? We'll have to carry on."

"Let's leave it in God's hands, this kind of thing happens.
Why did He take away this mum from her children?
They are yet but so small. It is so rough a spot.
So small! You can't tell them go work for your own lot."

"Go and bring them over. They must be scared alone,
Waking up to the sight of their mum who's long gone.
She now is calling us to shoulder her two kids,
Let us open our door, we'll have seven to feed"

"They'll grow up as siblings, playing all together,
Climbing over our laps like do any other.
We'll nourish them with love and fruits of our fishing
The good Lord will provide and more fish I will bring"

"When He sees us struggling at rearing this big bunch.
I will give it my best; at times I will skip lunch.
Ok. That's it! Go now, go fetch these poor angels.
But what's with you today? You're not one to fiddle…"

Heart pounding, jittery, Jeannie did not go far,
Pushing the dark curtain, she revealed: "Here they are!"

To the lovely Empress

*Love flies away
Far from the mind.
It is displayed
When two hands bind.*

*Just hear me say,
Do not give in
If I sigh, hey,
Keep on singing.*

*If I remain
Sad at your feet
And I complain
Laugh in a fit.*

*All men favor
A con artist
If I quaver
Just lose my piste.*

Idling

Rowing the river, a small boat
Glides over the waves aimlessly.
A fisherman stands by and gloats
At the boat riding saillessly.
With few shrugs he fixes his coat.

Early December on the land,
The souls are scarce in this forest.
The fisherman extends a hand
Balancing the rod at his best,
Patience comes out in great demand.

Flocks of swallows shift scenery.
The choice of trees just overwhelms,
No need to mark territory.
The fisherman adjusts his phlegm
As silent show of mastery.

And the small boat takes a last bow
To seemingly leave the waters,
Engulfed by the forest somehow.
This corner land is a shelter:
I think I will take a nap now.

But so it came, and so it goes,
I would love to keep the sketching.
But as in life, comes to a close
Whatever we hold as good thing.
I hope that this was one of those.

Even There

Gliding on north-east winds
Over the Whoestershades
Gladly the winter brings
The gleaming ice cascades.

They glow in the sunlight,
Melt in glossy surface
And holding branches tight
Make over Nature's face.

The glare of morning sun
Glitters like the season.
Whatever's left undone
Now has hidden reasons.

And the Noreaster blows,
Spreading chills, pouring rain
On all the souls below
Caught in Nature's refrain

For the years come and go
And along the seasons,
Solely conceived as though
His flock to cross bear none

But before soon arrives
Nature will recover
And again, come alive
And warm the air over.

Never any flower,
At given time to sprout,
Has failed to deliver
In good soil or in drought.

And the sun will project
The heat of every day
For its healing effect
From the Earth never sways.

Great's the variety
Offered to us humans
So that on the journey
Any trauma can mend.

All of our senses
Are challenged every day
Way above the fences
Of the downfalls at bay

For subtly, steadily
Over the centuries
God has so lovingly
Lulled all our worries.

A majestic sunrise,
A mountain in the fall
With shades that mesmerize
And hungry souls, enthrall.

Never a dull moment,
Not a high with no low,
Not a sweet endearment
Without a curséd blow.

So varied in essence
Is this our Nature
That always in a dance
She transports and nurtures.

Every living person
Who spurs from her bosom,
Can just bathe in her sun
From now till kingdom come.

She kisses and rewards
The ones who truly dare
To give sincere regards
To Love and all its glare.

Always at a set time
Comes to our rescue,
Like two nickels to dime
What to Nature is due.

Over the Whoestershades
Of every human soul
Nature depicts the shades
Of our lives as a whole.

And gladly the winds blow
Bringing us the seasons
While on us here below
Dawn the rays of the sun.

Nature in all aspects
Spreads around all the Love
Coming strong and direct
From the Father above.

Coward Thoughts

The things I could tell you
Remain stuck on my mind
Frozen dead by the view
Of your visage so fine.

The things I could tell you
Then are left unspoken
And form a lengthy queue
In my soul's secret den.

The things I could tell you
Gather other fierce thoughts
To come to their rescue
So they can break the knots,

And reach your lovely ears
In a sudden breakthrough,
And ridded of their fears
Tell you how I love you.

Depths of His Mercy

Silence, please set me a stage,
Need to scribble down my page
Cause I have so much I would like to tell,
I'd scream it out loud so they hear it well
For the world's in need and it has to hear.
Have no fear
Rest in the depths of His mercy.

But in my mind the words in race
Caused my pen not to keep the pace,
Words of wisdom made to ease the mind,
Words of purpose not so hard to find,
Words of solace like the ones He uttered so much
With His touch
Showing the depths of His mercy.

But as I closed my eyes I saw
Sentences following some law.
They were formed by a lonely finger,
In wild disarray they were no longer.
They were downpouring in the sound of a brook in Spring
Muffled strings
Echoing the depths of His mercy.

So skeptic, do you still deny,
Claiming that all is a big lie.
Hear His voice calling all His children,
Fill His touch among all the brethren,
Open up your heart so you can hear the call within,
Let Him in
And feel the depths of His mercy.

For the whole world now bows and prays
To the One God they have to praise
And my hand gladly feel up the page
With sentences like falling from the stage,
And voices like geysers shouting from the chest:
His Highest!
All for the depths of His mercy.

Inconsequences

In this rolling forsaken land of dust
What we deserve is fit for the unjust.
It overwhelms the quality of lust
That points all rights tucked under our pillows.

The repeated and flagrant disregard,
So many tugs at this tail of leopard
Causes this fright; our rightful reward.
More than ever we drown in our sorrow.

When the teachings relentlessly enounced
Will come out loud our ignorance denounce
Then history our sentence will pronounce
Which already this our era describes.

But as usual we remain deaf and dumb
In this obscure corridor that just numbs
Our common sense lacking like a sore thumb.
We disrespect the basic codes prescribed.

And we go on claiming all kind of rights.
We blame heaven, we blame left, we blame right.
The more we blame, the lesser we look bright
And farther we drift from the remedy.

But we're living the just consequences
Of our failures called inconsequences
We spread around breaking all defenses,
Those spiritual and those of the body.

The Night HE Was Betrayed

His last supper ending, the good Lord took the bread,
Alluding to His death, He broke it with his Hands.
"My life no one takes it, I freely give it instead
To ransom my people from the foe of this land."

His last meal all consumed, the dear Lord humbly went,
And offered His body to be slain on the Cross.
"My Blood is libation for the brand-new covenant
My friends, do this always, safe from memory loss."

As for us, God's people, we can freely proclaim
Your death, O Lord Jesus, by this bread and this wine.
Your church on bended knees Your resurrection acclaims,
You went all victorious to your glory divine.

Your living sacrifice of Eucharistic bread
Will quell deep in our hearts any spring of evil.
We are pure reflection of the divine light You shed
Help us always ward off all our lives upheaval.

O Lord, we patiently hope for Your great return
To take us all with You to Your supreme glory.
Your divine Love for us, as an eternal flame, burns,
Inviting Your children to behold Your story.

Under His Wings

Burdens, from up a tree galore,
Will fall not as a metaphor
And submerge you as an encore
Like refrain in this life you live.

Tribulations will come abound,
Soaring from within your mind ground
Surprisingly without a sound,
The peace in you just to deceive.

And when weary you'll try to find
Solace from someone of your kind,
In turn they'll put you in a bind,
Sometimes not voluntarily.

You'll have recourse to the Father,
Hoping one way or another,
To give you help He will bother
But all status quo quietly.

Regardless of your shortcoming,
Regardless how late your blessing,
Regardless how overwhelming
Is your stress you should rest assured,

Never has His kindness left you,
Never has His Spirit failed you,
Never has He forgotten you.
HE shoulders all that you endure.

One day how would you really feel,
When your journey comes to stand still
To look up and to take a fill
Of the weight of this blessed truth?

And realize that all along,
All with His arm mighty and strong
That He brought you where you belong,
When at His Face you always hoot.

Your spirit being a part of Him
Has to be taken to the gym
Where tribulations are the themes
Set to make you strong in His eyes.

So when under your wood don't mope.
Success' always an upward slope.
HE's with us with all that we cope.
HE never once severed the ties.

Relax

And the whole world is tumbling down
Or so you think, my dear,
He replied first, with a deep frown.
The set order of things remains.
Oh don't have any fear
The clamor's shouted rather often.

Nothing escapes the One in charge,
Nothing that lives and breathes.
And what you see that now just barged
Has for so long deceived
A great many generations
With the vilest of intentions.

It would be wrong to say to you
There should be no concern
When everywhere you see those who
Sadly succumb to the stealth foe
That they could not discern
Because of what they did not know.

Take a good look at what's around
And remain unafraid.
Keep your head high, feet on the ground
And of your heart open the doors
And allow love to raid
As in the deadliest of scare.

Life Choices

The aftermath of good old days
Come crashing heavy on our lawn.
They never hear the words we say,
Warning them from day until dawn.

The sunny days that they enjoy
Selfishly blind their common sense
So they go everywhere and toy,
Spreading disaster and offence.

Like donkey in room full of eggs,
Their least move causes disaster.
And they roam around like a plague
Though they mourn the sad thereafter.

If God's willing they crash early,
Blessings bestow us anytime,
They quickly stand and learn sadly
That Love with freedom does not rhyme.

So at the end of the charade,
When nothing is what should have been,
We get memories as a trade,
Bitterly missing the old scene.

Along The Way

The passing time and strolling years
From all around will gather fears
Wrenching from missing all our peers
Who left along the way.

They blaze the trail for our sorrow,
Truly shying their tomorrow,
Leaving us stranded here below,
Struggling along the way.

Beyond veil of uncertainty,
The silent foe's dark enmity
With infernal facility
Engulfs along the way

The predestined legion of us
Who planned a life so longevous
But failed to sense the non-obvious
Which came along the way.

Earth more than once suffered all this
But emerged with a touch of bliss,
Healing her wounds, filling her miss,
Spinning along the way.

It fits and so this I repeat,
The relentless human spirit
Will always land back on its feet
Spring forth along the way.

Surrender

If you want to drink from the well,
The well of the true living God,
Depart from where your free will dwells
Enter in the sweet divine pod.

If you don't surrender your life
Under the Will of the dear Lord,
Your concern or your inner strife
Will never bring you true accord.

To the doors of heavenly bliss,
No one reaches until they plead
"Lord let thy will be all I miss",
"Ignore the echo of my greed!"

God wants to put a brand-new soul
Within you, if you let Him in.
Take up your cross and pay the toll
Giving Him glory deep within.

If you surrender all, wholly,
You'll win the Heart of your Savior.
Creator and creature slowly
Divine Love will come to savor.

From this bond sealed from up above
Will trickle truly bléssed fruits:
You will do all that the Lord loves,
HE will bless all of your pursuits.

Stillness

In the thunder of the tomb
Where silence is deafening
Never resound of the womb
The clamors of the hearing.

Every inch of quiescence,
Every note of tune unsung,
Every minute of absence
Underscores where you belong.

Never was it a mistake,
Never a minute ahead.
Never a regret at stake;
The world remains on its stead.

Time's given to examine
The longest string of should've
But what's left remains unseen:
The large realm of the could've.

You fly to settle accounts
In your land of ancestors.
To what it really amounts
Can at times mean disaster.

There, the thunder of the tomb
With silence still deafening,
Always resound from the womb
Loud clamors of all sobbing.

The Journey

I can attest that this journey
Although for some of us gruesome,
As perilous as it may come
Remains precious to so many.

They lovingly give of their best
Sharing the little they may have,
Even acting on the behalf
Of those they see treading unrest.

They travel safely with the rule
That only what you sow you reap
And so give kindness in a heap
Although the world sees them as fools.

Along their journey they apply
The principles that they endear.
It's the law whose goal is to veer
Away from them the slick and sly.

*Deliver what you don't receive,
Always give more than what you're asked.
Of false pretense don't wear a mask
But your heart carry on your sleeve.*

*The blows to you will be many
And they will surge from everywhere
But deep inside the love you wear
Will secure safely your journey.*

*And always rooted on the prize,
The utmost of inspirations
Despite the many commotions
Keep steady the fix of your eyes.*

*And soon you'll see that this journey,
As treacherous as it can be,
Is but what you want it to be:
The essence of your destiny.*

It's Time

Free from within you all aspects
Of this agnostic debonair
Whose soul suffered the wear and tear
Of the dots he failed to connect.

Life will offer loads of reasons
To dock your canoe where it fits.
Your inner compass will defeat
All drifting over your seasons.

So settle down while time's at hand
You never know the reaching foe
That can burst any tomorrow
And sneak you into its own land

And shed the once upon a time,
The petty settings of your mind.
Your life itself will not be kind
If you were to forfeit your prime.

Calmly

Oh how I long for the day,
The day solemn, the day bright,
Day that'd mark the silent night
With souvenirs on its sleigh.

Day traveling through all time
And compelling to the mind,
Redirecting to the blind
All the brooks of scent of thyme.

It will surely set ashore
The dreaded reasons to be
And the waves of all the seas
Will sing calmly as before.

Even the moon of spindle
With a crest of long ago
Will acapella solo
The treasures of its jingle.

So before it all resumes
To the point way far beyond
The whole world upon its pond
Will forever gladly spume.

No Longer

I went straight ahead, blindfolded,
With my heart on my sleeve, loaded,
And belittling the great unknown,
With my wooden king to enthrone.

In the mirage of my desert
I jumped right in like no expert,
Assuming that you had a heart
But you were playing from the start.

The solemn words I disavow,
The ones exchanged between the sobbing tears,
For all reasons somehow,
I just keep asking how
One could lie to anyone so dear.

My words repeated to your ears
Were uttered to erase the fear
I thought I saw in your brown eyes
But they shadowed a pack of lies.

Now when alone I think all through
And how my dream never came true
I jump right back in my deep sleep,
Afraid to reality leap.

No longer will I fall in love,
No longer will I stand the endearments,
The trauma that they shove
Within me when heard of
Is to me source of all torments.

But now I left the world behind,
Finally freed up from the bind
At a price I could not afford:
My poor heart every broken cord.
No longer will I fall in love.

The Ears

Ears on the run did you hear roar
The Voice of God in His thunder?
Around the world the timbers soar,
Relentless barks put asunder
Your inner peace and its décor.

Ears on the run did you recall
The truth so often repeated?
They try to spare you from the fall
Keeping your world so elated,
That same output you appall.

Ears on the run try not to dwell
On the precept asperities.
They're made the body needs to quell
With love and just severity
For the flow of sin not to swell.

Ears on the run you should instead
Run convey them to the others.
This way their spirits will be fed,
On their journey they'll go farther
And they'll recant the dirt they spread.

Ears on the run if only you
Should ponder on the importance
Of every word Heaven made to
Save you from cheap interference
You would follow them all way through.

Ears on the run it's sad to see
How your kind does but pick and choose
Which leaves their souls at the mercy
Of the con artist on the loose
And of trouble bring them a sea.

Ears on the run every precept
Have been divinely mastermind'
To tackle the many concepts
That in human life you may find,
This truth your world will not accept.

Ears on the run can you fathom
The chaos all over the world,
The pain provoked by the gruesome
Flow that all the blasphemes unfurl
As a presage of things to come?

Ears on the run heed the warnings.
They come pressing, with silent cries.
They see the tears and sufferings,
Results of severing the ties
With the Source of life indwelling.

The Sound of Solitude

The peaceful sound of solitude
A great many of us eludes.
It requires an attitude
That always scares the mass away.

The peaceful sound of solitude
Rolls down from this long habitude
Of retiring in one's etude
To read, to write, ponder and pray.

The peaceful sound of solitude
Will entice some dudettes and dudes
Thus demeaning pleasures preclude,
Bring much precious knowledge their way.

The peaceful sound of solitude
Offers wisdom in plenitude
To those willing to self-seclude
Thus to the spiritual world sway.

The Great "I AM"

In the midst of thy darkest night,
In the midst of thy wretched fright,
Right deep in thy most silent night,
There I shall be.

And there, unaware and so weak,
Thou being so gentle and meek,
The enemy with claws and beak
Shall gnash at thee.

Never shall thou know the attack,
Never shall thou sense any crack,
Never, since all beyond thy back,
All these take scene.

For thou art never left alone,
Never shall any stick or stone
Come harm thy rest, supine or prone,
Nor on thee lean.

Tis my promise I make to thee.
In thy mind doubt should never be,
Proof of the Love I have for thee
Till end of time.

So that thou know deep in thy heart
And that thou so loudly impart,
Sing to the world "How great Thou art".
The great "I AM".

Silent Promise

In a course of my dreary day,
Amidst all that can go astray,
Between the sneaky come-what-may,
There, on my knees my mind remains.

I know things just can't be rosy.
He promise us there'll be many
Of these days cloudy and rainy
But sunrays we'll always regain.

But deep in my supplication
I beg the Lord to take action
And from this bondage free His son
But I still hear the same refrain:

"Though the sea waves rage their fury",
Though the wind blows loud and eerie",
Though lightning destroys mighty trees"
My grace will soothe your every pain".

"Deep within you where I abide,"
Deep within you I never chide".
Deep within you I see you tried"
So many times on this journey".

"But in the crush of your sorrow"
Where you shed your tears in a row"
You wash your soul so tomorrow"
You'll hold again your dear Junie".

Sacred Heart of JESUS

O blessèd Heart of my Savior,
You, of every life, the Author
Make that we look upon Your glow
And on us here Your candor sow
For this journey so rich in love
You invite us to be part of.

Upon your chest, beating and bright.
It shines Your Love and Mercy's light,
For this our faith, ablaze beacon
And for hope, an anchor thereon,
This shimmering Heart where Your Love
Secures our help from up above.

O blessèd Heart of my Savior,
With Your grace do our hearts over.
Gather all the souls of the world
In Your sweet Love like precious pearls,
That every nation lives compelled
To march with Your Gospel upheld.
Amen!

MARY, Mother of Love

Blesséd Mother of Love
Guide us along our way.
Your shining light, we pray,
Gleam on us from above.

Heal us Blesséd Mother,
From ills of our seasons.
We bring you our sick ones,
Their agony, smother.

At the foot of the cross
With faith you stood in pain.
Close to us please remain
To sanctify our loss.

Gift to humanity,
You do know all our needs.
Just as Cana, please feed
Our lot of charity.

Help us, Mother of Love,
The Father's will to heed
And thus we'll live the Creed
Led by the Holy Dove.

The Lord in His Goodness
Took away all our sins.
Pray that we'll be all seen
Caught in Heaven's gladness.

Amen!

Prayer to The Immaculate Conception of MARY

Oh pray, dear Mother, for us all,
Of the world deign to hear the call,
Down on its knees from all the falls
It suffered from the dawn of time,

Misery and sheer injustice,
Hatred and violence in our midst,
Terror and wars to top all these;
Because we shun the Great "I AM".

Deign with the Holy Rosary,
To help us, O Mother Mary
To grasp the blesséd mysteries
Of He, source of our divine peace.

Help us dear Mother to become
Living channels of His Kingdom,
Bringing solace to our fewsome
As a foretaste of Heaven's bliss.

Of our planet so desolate,
Blessed Mother, please mourn the fate.
Here, where your dear Son trod of late,
Pray to ward off all wretchedness.

Please, pray for us, Mother of Hope,
Give us peace so that we can cope.
And when from here we should elope
We'll see your Son in blessédness.

Amen!

See

See how the peaceful dusk painted by the red sun
Leaves your soul imprinted with melancholic fits.
Hear the far away call of your lulled-up spirit
Reminding your ego of marvels it once shunned.

See how the rolling sea with unrelented waves
Seems to try to reshape the surface of the dune.
See the message offered amid this steady tune
To never give up hope till you cuddle the grave.

See the human spirit soaring against all odds
To reach the peaceful glow surging from pure wisdom.
They carry their crosses yearning for His Kingdom
Though never in their lives they once walked where He trod.

See the magical glow the moon over nature
Spreads ever silently; nightly loving caress.
Nature flirtatiously her trenches let impress
And spends most of her nights inert in this rapture.

See the change of seasons with no notion of time
Set nature steadily and so ever slowly,
All for the excitement of your brown eyes to see
Till Autumn comes ashore and then with your heart rhyme.

Softly And Gently

Softly and gently the Lord will carry
Each and every soul riding His mercy.
Softly and gently, they are so many
Still in dire need of His liturgy.

Do onto others as you would do you,
Carry your own load of burden daily.
What is your brother's you should not envy,
May you daily deeds to your heart be true.

Softly and gently of the so many
The Lord of spirits feeds the hearts daily
Through the frequent read of His liturgy,
Softly and gently He shows His mercy.

Writing

I'm writing still just as before,
Writing my life, writing galore,
Sprinkling it with some metaphors,
Trying to get my point across.

I'm writing still, writing encore,
Writing of the change of decors
Each time that life knocks at my door,
Proving to me who is the Boss.

But then through all turmoil I write,
Often when my sky's not so bright,
Over some point to shed some light
I run to scribble down my voice.

And when all will be said and done,
Of string of words there'll be left none
I will beg to be left alone
To still tackle my task of choice.

From The Start

I will attempt with pen in hand,
To shed some light on this subject,
And hopefully you'll understand
What of this life you should expect.

I'd compare any love affair
To a seed planted in the soil.
It will grow strong, if given care,
To face upcoming stress and toil.

But from the start you should invest
The love you plan to reap after
For from the start it will ingest
Every ounce of pain or laughter.

Do not expect that a cold ring
Will come and change your behavior,
And do not think that at signing
You'll get some love from the Savior.

From the get go you should enforce
All measures designed to construct
A love no deep-rooted remorse
Will come molest or just destruct.

In all occasion show your care,
Do not play cool with your feelings.
Invite your love to come and share
Your life in all aspects of things.

Invest your love in the Springtime
To ensure your Summer and Fall.
With every nickel, every dime,
Winter will see your love grow tall.

Nothing you should take for granted,
Everything scars a growing flame.
At times they'll think you're demented
But show your passion just the same.

So come with your love loud and clear,
Put your universe at her feet.
Slowly you will entice your dear,
Slowly you'll breathe the same spirit.

The treasure that is sought after,
Source of your deep, unspoken dreams,
Is worth that daily you swelter
To reach that goal you so esteem.

And see your love grow deep and strong,
Even beyond your wildest dreams.
Love always docks where it belongs,
It always hears the silent screams.

One Sad Day

*Can I reveal to you, my dear
How much I miss you over here?
How I remain under your spell
So deep my words can't even tell?*

*No, no my friend, it's illegal,
She replied, but not so frugal…
Then I thank God for then I saw
The heart remains under no law.*

The Old Square

At dawn in the early morning,
When life runs out of all feelings
And comes rebound as a sure thing,
Then springs alive the old hotel.

Every living soul in a rush
Guardedly surfs on the big slush,
Carefully holding to their plush
En route to the square Solenstel.

Amid the many who reside,
In the suburb, on the far side,
They follow the sun as a guide
And gladly head on towards East.

For tomorrow they celebrate
Unlike some unknown twist of fate
Their holiday sent not too late,
Their blessed Nahka Basha feast.

And all around the square they go.
They tread in-group or go solo
And their footsteps sharply echo
In the misty morn on the square.

The silent words that they exchange
Seem to suddenly rearrange
Their trajectory. It's so strange
To witness such a thoroughfare.

Aftermath

Though I had a sleepless night,
Thank you for being so nice.
They were folded, so neet, so right,
Wish this could happen to me twice.

Written to someone after they folded my clothes collected by mistake the night before.

O Blesséd FATHER

Lord of hosts to You we come,
At Your feet this early dawn
To offer from the bosom
All that today's to be drawn.
O blesséd Father

Humbly Lord we beseech You
For our sins be merciful.
Show Your kindness to those who
Fail though they'd be not spiteful.
O blesséd Father

You who so much sustain us,
Who know well our weakness
Make us evermore pious
And quell our wretchedness
O blesséd Father

Lord, You solemnly promise;
If united we remain,
Praying You for what we miss
We'll be heard from Your Mountain
O blesséd Father

Therefore we joyfully bring
To Your altar this clear day,
Voices with fervent hymns sing
And deep love to send Your way
O blesséd Father.

Holy Trinity

Bless the Lord forever
HE forgets us never.
With His almighty Hand
HE protects and commands.
HE sees deep in the hearts,
Won't let them break in parts.

Love the Lord forever
HE betrays us never.
With His love and power
Came down as our Savior
To guide us with His light,
Make us just in God's sight.

Trust the Lord forever
HE gave us His power,
That strong Spirit in us
Making us wise and just.
HE dwells in us and stays
Till the end of our days.

Psalm 27

The Lord is my light and my salvation.
On this long journey, of whom should I fear?
He is my refuge as long as I'm here,
I live unafraid, in sweet devotion.

Just one thing I ask, just one thing I seek;
Into His abode to live all my days
So that I rapture in gazing His way,
And see His temple, strong and majestic.

O hear, blessed Lord, the sound of my call.
Have pity on me, please answer my plea.
Of You my heart speaks, You I long to see,
Don't cast me away, lest I trip and fall.

You are my Helper, abide with me Lord,
In your sweet Heaven unveil your bounty.
I wait unafraid, O Lord Almighty,
I wait stouthearted; I'll wait for my Lord.

Advent Antiphon

Rejoice my dear, rejoice,
Let them all hear your voice.
Your God, the Almighty,
Has shown you His mercy.
He'll lift you up, my dear,
Of your trials have no fear.
He'll sweep you up your feet
And perk up your spirit.

For painful centuries
You longed for His mercies.
Today your time has come,
No more you'll be loathsome.
For the King of all kings,
Of David's upbringing,
The mighty Counselor,
Robed in all His grandeur,
Will come walk on your land.
So rejoice, rejoice then.

Jesus Christ

Jehovah, we praise you,
Everlasting pleasure.
Supreme God, we love You
Unfaltering treasure
Source of covenant new.

Creator ingenuous,
Harbor of divine grace,
Righteous in all Your ways,
Indwelling all of us.
Spirit who never sways,
Teacher of human race.

The Lasting Impression

The lasting impression of any given act
Lies in circumstances backing up its impact.
It's never visible, not even palpable
But its effect remains nonetheless bearable.

The lasting impression is given like a seal
On the soul of the one who harbors it a feel.
It lingers a somewhat, steadily permeates
All facets of the life it sets to dominate.

The lasting impression leaches on silently
Night and day, by the hand it leads the psyche on.
Affecting the strata, underlying trenches,
Just like slow-falling snow on all the tree branches.

The lasting impression, depending on its source,
Will dictate naturally of its victim the course.
It comes as a warning, a clue, a presentment
But will ring your mind's ears at the proper moment.

The lasting impression therefore should be welcome
For it will never fail to warn the dear fewsome
Who during their lifetime succumbed in the action
And received, good or bad, its tattooed sensation.

Contemplation

Peep at a young girl as she bathes
Robed only with her innocence,
Watch sails whose keels the blue sea lave,
Gape at the night sky bright stars pave,
See lawn worms shine in their nuisance.

Watch dance around gloomy statues
Sultanas in their fleeting veils,
See girandoles with dazling hues,
Night gondolas glide from your view,
Of shooting stars follow the trail.

Gaze at the ever serene moon,
Rest in tree shades on long journeys,
Thrill the whole world with just one tune
When this lovely air that you croon
Blesses souls as brings you money.

Listen from a harp melody
The sorrows of an old romance,
Wander with heart in rahpsody
Seeing throng of lovely ladies
Move each to her charming cadence.

Ponder as the dew of the dawn
Rains down the landscape of your dream,
While the notes that nightingales spawn,
Trickling down gladly on your lawn,
Igniting fires of your steam.

Blot out of your mind all the years,
Every old dream and its misstep,
Follow the trail, devoid of fear,
Of any genie or its peer,
As it sheds light at each footstep.

All golden buds that the spring sheds
Over the green of charming lawn,
Glimpse, after long exile in stead,
Your home town church while being led
Through trails of love that April spawns.

All that the future has in store,
All that is true and mesmerize
Rhymes to nothing within my core
When over me, lovely décor,
Gently you set your loving eyes.

The Young Girl

Just yesterday, through my window,
My eyes scoping, vaguely seeing
Fell on a girl, svelte as a doe,
In the Marne, gleeful rags, washing.

Near the old bridge, amid willows,
She washed and washed and came and went.
The breeze of dawn came to borrow
Some of the grace she had to vent.

From afar I saw her mantis
Dancing at the wave of the wind.
It joined the shrubs in waving bliss
In the balmy air of the spring,

The bushes shoved by gentle breeze
That May and June, jolly daubers,
Crushing the tank of sap with ease,
Spread with a large coat of flowers,

Elderberries with waves of flies,
To border brooms, of any kind,
To rushes reflecting their size
In the green flow that runs and winds.

She kept hanging pure white tatters,
A whole bunch of old charming rags
That she, among branches, scattered,
With glow that under the sun bragged.

All these clothes in the golden dawn,
Seemed, under the alder and birch,
Favor Kythira's lovely swans
Fanning their wings right where they perch.

Cupid with his plan to entice,
Exposed her pink and slender feet.
Her dress folded up once or twice
Displayed her lovely white legs' split.

You could see, seriously speaking,
Much higher than above her knees.
From under the vine, recurring,
Some cow bellowed: Caution, warning!

I left my room at the small Inn,
And walked with a plan to the bank,
Like a hunter with senses keen,
With the weather and birds to thank.

I looked at her, free of disdain
As I leaned against the birch trunk
And told her: "My lovely maiden!
(Young girl, would have made me a punk)

"Birds are chirping and the lamb bleats,
What luck for this remote quarter!
My maiden, at your lovely feet,
I came for your smile to barter.

"I can sit here for the whole day
For just like the warblers hover,
I'll wait, my maiden till you say,
That now my love search is over.

"For so long I have dreamed of this,
Amid roses, in early spring,
That love would come crash with its bliss
On riverbank while nature sings.

"Kings of all sort fight fearlessly
For maidens as lovely as you.
The Marne now flows effortlessly
Just cause you came its zest renew.

"O maiden with loveliest feet,
He, who loves you, is rich indeed.
If you so desire I'll just sit
Till with your smile my heart you feed."

And the jolly, charming young girl
Giggled but from the house next door
Her parents, from their lovely pearl,
Missed the beater unlike before.

Old folks will thunder and then scold
But us the youth we always dare.
A kiss often comes quick and bold
Once sweet glances and smile are paired.

I'll stop at this. It's ill fitted
To reminisce and go too deep.
A kiss rightfully merited
Leads minds to what Heavens safe keeps.

An evening, in sowing season

At these hours of the twilight,
I admire, from the front gate,
This end of day's fading sunlight,
The end of work on the estate.

On the land with rising shadows,
Moved, I can see the ragged clothes
Of an old man who calmly throws
The future harvest that he chose.

His tall silhouette from afar
Towers over the well-tilled fields.
All rest upon, what is so far,
The result that only time yields.

He paces the immense meadow,
Goes back and forth, steady seeder,
Goes on steady amid the rows
And I ponder, silent seer,

While the evening, spreading its veils
Of shadows where mingle soft sounds,
Seems of his gestures leave a trail
Reaching the stars right from the ground.

Song

The swallows have all departed.
The hay nests shiver on the roofs.
Nettles of water are plated.
Good lumberjack, don't be aloof.

The swallows have all departed.
The air is cold, the hearth is warm.
Nettles of water are plated.
Good collier, bring your coal to farm.

The swallows have all departed.
Summer traipses its warmth away.
Nettles are still water-plated.
Bundle maker, bring us your hay.

The swallows have all departed.
Hello, winter, farewell, blue sky!
Nettles of water are plated.
If you feel cold, set your hearth high.

The swallows have all departed.
Frosty the nights, breezy the days.
All nettles are water-plated.
You, the living, cuddle away.

The hydra

When the son of Sancha, wife of the duke Geoffrey,
Gil, this great knight they named everywhere Man of steel,
Ended with spear held up and visor down and still,
Went deep in the country Ramire rendered free,

He saw the hydra there, majestic and frightening,
Lying under the sun, daydreaming in the grass.
The knight pulled up his sword. "Tis I", he said, with class,
The hydra stood up then, from one mouth, height stretching,

And said: "Why did you come, you, Doña Sancha's son,
Is it for me, say, or for Ramire, the king"?
"I came for the monster. – Then Sir, it's a sure thing,
You want the king". Slowly, to its daydream went on.

Charade

The gloom over me hazing
Grimaces at every tone
Of this tune I try to sing
For when majesty's dethrone'
The court then does its own thing.

Sadly, there's not a fiber,
Not an ounce in nowadays
To slip a shade of laughter
But hope is a dawn away
To the faithful believer.

No need to misplace the goal
That faithful prayer will reach.
There will be always a toll,
The believer finds a breach
If he looks deep in his soul.

But never there is a need
To holler the naked truth,
It is well known in its seed.
The fairy needs just one tooth
To spread around her good deeds.

Sipping slowly at this gall
You will taste the love you miss.
But won't hear her silent call
For alone in your abyss
You can see dusk slowly fall.

Always in other quarters
Short of rain there is blue sky.
Staring down the hereafter
You can see your life zoom by,
No time left for your barter.

Right there class, gender and race
All aspects of divergence
On your screen come show their face.
Every so upheld difference
Of importance lost all trace.

This song I refrain deep down
Well caught up within my cage
To my neighbor brings a frown
For every willing hostage
To the world favors a clown.

Nothing in life is secure.
You may win or you may lose.
But always what you endure
To the gander or the goose
Offer as sheer literature.

Love hides no cacophony
Once it invites us to dance.
Blessed are the so many
Who at its treasure took glance,
For this I thank my Junie.

The Final Point

Excuse the casual bother
From my dragging, muffled dirge.
But sad words from a brother,
That recurrently emerge
Should be dealt with much smoother.

Never is there any sense
For laughter to be at bay.
When purging for one's offense
It is so futile to say
That prayer is not worth pence.

Should I mourn or should I laugh,
Is the choice offered to me.
Misleading would be the path
That adopts polygamy
As a scornful epitaph.

Rather focus on the how
To shout out your contentment
And still poker face somehow.
Just like at the interment
Of a foe you long avow'.

He who once tangoed with love
And reclined at its table
Rightfully will always shove
The sound of any fable
If not sent from high above.

Look around and try gather
A makeshift for your pleasure
And your bliss, push much farther.
Never one should go measure
The wisdom of another.

Peacefully the horizon,
If peered at so intensely
Will spit much-needed seasons,
Maybe not so hurriedly,
To rear all daughters and sons.

But all remains out of sight,
Like an over-used adage
Your intelligence to slight.
And all alone on your stage
Your rendition loses might.

And you're faced in your silence
With ideas that gone astray
From fear of your rude cadence
That chased all their drives away.
How baffling for your audience!

Only one chance is given
To the soul to be complete
And all its scores to even.
When on Earth you fail to meet
You unite in God's heaven.

Shut the door right to my face,
Burn the book if you see fit.
Nothing will ever erase
The true north of my spirit
And off-track him on his chase.

Once quenched from this living stream,
One will shun a stagnant pond.
Once love held you in esteem,
No one, nor brunette nor blond
Will take her place in your dream.

My first verse, her brown eyes spew'
Tumbling down, chiseling my page,
Opening a realm brand new
Where my world lies in bondage,
Praying my dream will come true.

Wintry Nightfall

Right above in the eventide
Take a load of this crimson sky.
Heavy clouds appear and then glide
But not a pair of wings fly by.
Seems like winter's here to abide.

But all along the winding road
Traces of wildlife linger on.
And the few holes bunnies burrowed
Are concrete signs of the season
When hunger is the only load.

The incandescent orange ball
Lost its power over the eyes,
In the sky stands no longer tall
But now has a reddened disguise
While sustaining its last free fall.

But who minds the light in the sky,
Who will affix its evening glow?
Who would replace or even try
To shine instead till tomorrow,
When half the world in silence lies.

Life in its essence takes a pause,
All clamors fall in decibels.
The guilty partner pleads its cause,
The tocsin soars from the chapel.
All energies decline in dose.

A softer glow now permeates
Every trench of Mother Nature
And over the snowy estate
All indulge in nightly leisure
Or pray for a change of their fate.

A radio shouts in the cold air
The reggae sound of an artist.
A puppy relentlessly dares
To scare some stranger from its list
Its vocal cords it doesn't spare.

In the indigo sky above
Flickering glows reflect away.
They display lovely shape of clove
But at times one shoots on its way
Wishing good cheers to each alcove.

As the night soothes their every ill
And the moon placates with her glow,
Over the world where life stands still
All hopes await for tomorrow
For every soul to get their fill.

And dreams come kiss every forehead
Eager to sweep the souls away.
While eyelids weigh their ton of lead
And the good deeds of this today
Sing lullaby and rock the beds.

The night returns to weary souls
The just reaping of their sowing.
All done under karma's control,
All done amidst of loud snoring;
Justice always collects its toll.

The cold glides over the valley,
Gripping and the frail and the strong,
Silently shunning the tally
Of perpetrators' right or wrong,
In here just as in Italy.

Still in the air softly blowing
Disrupted flakes fly here and there.
The wind prevents them from resting
After this long free fall affair
From mother cloud bondage tearing.

Tree branches so heavy laden
Dream of the rising of the sun
To melt the snow, in slow sudden.
From the snow fall they are still stun',
Hanging from morning until then.

A stray dog turns around the bench
Heading for a pile of wastage
To then quickly go down the trench
Holding a scary toad hostage.
A big snowball falls off a branch.

Down there, in the obscure valley
Where the soundless world is breathing
The chests exhale much heavily
The life of which they know nothing
Taking with grunts so noisily.

And so it goes with eyes ablaze
You can scope all over the town
For sure you won't see any haze
But everything wears a snow crown,
This status quo will be for days.

Right above in this early dawn
Take a load of the sky above.
Heavy clouds still over the lawn,
Birds alike behaving as dove,
All as winter remains in fawn.

Bare Ceiling

My mind's loaded with thoughts at hand:
Should I answer, should I ignore
You gently knocking at my door…

Or should I go on and pretend
That all is well, that as before
You are the only thought I bore…

But now things changed, they always do,
A new day for us just broke dawn.
Though I chose to stay home and yawn
I will dispell the thoughts of you.

What Does His Love Trigger in You

What does His love trigger in you?
End of this old-world shut and tight
Or full of hope, maybe it might
Get all the hearts to love anew
End up all fights
What does His love trigger in you?

What does His love trigger in you?
The young untouched by the obscene
Praying that hope should intervene.
The love and hate that we once knew
No more is seen
What does His love trigger in you?

What does His love trigger in you?
Tight fists against every struggle
But when you press the right toggle
You change the scenery right through,
Your mind boggles
What does His love trigger in you?

What does His love trigger in you?
My dear nothing lasts forever
Lady luck favors whoever
Can get to kiss her feet beaucoup,
Seek them wherever
What does His love trigger in you?

What does His love trigger in you?
A better ending for all deals
Since the hearts aren't made of steel
Much better ones are made anew
Keep loving still
What does His love trigger in you?

Ode to Erato

Come in and hear the sound.
This sound muffled out loud,
This cry I don't emit
That I spill at your feet.

In me anchored deeply
I silence my folly
For in the crimson sky
I long to watch you fly.

You my muse, you my life
Who knows my every strife
Come and take possession
Of my deep emotions.

I want to feel you breathe,
From you my life, retrieve.
You lead my every way,
I pine when you're away.

Whenever you're around
Love within me abounds.
You stroke my very soul
With words I don't control.

For all over my plains
Where echoes your refrain
The seasons come and go
And always melts the snow.

So come and step right in
Build me from deep within.
Be it night, be it day
I heed the words you say.

Be the sole driving force,
The silent code of Morse
And shed at a mere call
All the leaves of my fall.

And South bound all the birds
Directed by your words
Convey in jovial screams
Their ways to warmer streams.

Every word, every thought
All within my lines caught,
Lovingly gets to drag
The colors of your flag.

And you stroll up and down
All the streets of my town,
And my forest lingers,
For your prance it hungers.

When you step on my sand
I can see wonderland.
In my stories of bliss
Your name once was Alice.

You don't ever recess,
At any time caress
My mind, your sole playground
Though you don't make a sound.

The stars gleaming at night
Rekindle at your sight
The zest of their fire
So they can shoot higher.

Be the source of my themes,
The sole mate of my team
Who fashions all my lines
And their cadence defines.

And there, between the lines
I spot my glass of wine.
Half empty or half full,
Nonetheless a mere tool

For my world is at peace
In such a trade as this.
You lead all the actions
And I pay attention.

Alone in my alcove
I honor my sweet dove.
And my world standing still,
Always streams down your will.

Never Can Say

Slowly slowly we drift apart,
Nothing remains from the old dart
Of love given to us so long ago.
Within my arms where you linger,
Silently nursing my sorrow,
Your kindness I get no longer.

Slowly, slowly right at the seams
We come apart as it all seems,
Bright sun to its chamber retiring.
Rocking away the good old days,
More then often reminiscing
When a ginger comes in to play.

Slowly, slowly I try to say
But words I call to come and play
Remain caught up in far away seasons.
I dread that the night suddenly
Would rob me from my last reason
Causing me to wreck mentally.

Slowly, slowly when all is gone
And the memories all come undone
Playing hide and seek with actuality.
Remains the painful commotion
When the mind shoves reality
To entertain its own notion.

What a Life

Entertaining a few good friends
The passing seasons as a trend
Contagious laughter of children
A heartache every now and then.
Taking a long walk on the beach
A helping hand within your reach
A free good meal when you're hungry
Sincere amend when you're angry.

The early warm days of the spring
And the buds of flower they bring
The fresh air caressing your face
Your loved one safe in your embrace.
So much that we take for granted
That in our lives have been planted
Like a taste for melodious strings
When in your ears a symphony rings.

A quiet room and a warm bed
After your day heavy as lead
From afar a car horn blowing
At the dawn your coffee sipping
Finally reaching a cool shade
Walking down a sunny parade
Lend a hand to a friend in need
And watch their burden away speed.

Pacing lightly on a crowded street
See lovely faces here and there to greet
Good food coking in the air rising
On a quiet day of glorious spring
To all these blessings once ignored
All emanating from the dear Lord
Are what makes life a blessed breeze
When at last their meanings we seize.

Made in Heaven

Come glide between my words, bring life to my meters,
Every shade I utter, every rhyme thereafter.
I your generic stream clothe me with sense and soul,
I want to rise and swirl, exposing the untold.

Born I was to convey many revelations.
Born I was to instill the print of emotions.
With you my better half, my jolly attire
I sense within my words the warmth of your fire

Music will you marry, do solemnly avow,
Poem will you cherish, until then and from now
And now I do declare. To the world take a bow.

Be my world, I am soil, be my world, you're the rain.
Sprout away my essence buried in your refrain.
I can sit on a page for so great many years
But with you in my words I can reach many ears.

Together we can rise and feed revolutions.
When the ears catch the air we seal the attentions.
We are the vocal stairs on which glide the spirits
When lonely and famished they crave for divine treats.

I promise I will be forever your shadow
Though I may land my rhymes to two, three in a row.
I will always remain fitted within your score
To happily be sung to crowds as an encore.

You vibrate all my words, resounding all my rhymes,
Exposing all my soul made bare time after time.
Whenever I feel lost I rely on your beat,
Heaven's always so near when you and I we meet.

The Tales of The Deep Sea

*The sea is the witness
Of its great tragedies
Though it never confess'
Any of its stories.*

*The sea rocks all the dreams
Of all generations
Whether or not they're deemed
Fitted for naration.*

*The sea fashions the wings
Of imagination
But gives silent blessings
To abominations.*

*The tales of the deep sea
Is not of sand and stone,
Nor of all the algae
That thus far we have known.*

*The sea is above all
The source of reveries,
The curtain of all calls
For great love penuries.*

*The sea often conceals
Of the world the mistakes
But chooses to reveal
Some for history sake.*

It rocks the cast away
For years and years after
But can sink any day
The greatest destroyer.

The tales of the deep sea
Tell of rolling rages
And with great secrecy
Surf through all the ages.

The sea is a blessing
Of survival at best,
Feeds the globe with all things
Caught right within her nest.

And it's the promise land
Where love cannot submerge,
Taking us by the hand
Rocking our every pledge.

The tales of the deep sea
Remains so far untold,
They have the buoyancy
Of waters made of gold.

The Being to Have

We want to be who has and be because we have,
We want to be who has, be just by what we have
But that really is vain enough,
Because we only have that what we truly are
If we are thus nothing or maybe not so much,
We have what we are, simply naught.

We only can be when we know well that we have,
We only can be when if truly it, we have.
If we believe to be only that what we have
Without minding the way that we are, and we have
So true value to them we freely can impart,
If we act otherwise, then we're wasting our time.
The other choice will be to have nothing or naught
Because the true value of to be and to have,
Results from strict exchange and the effort applied
In the being and the having

Their perfect harmony as the goal ought to be,
The unitive rapport, sole aim has always been:
There we go, God simply,
Yes, just God, actively!

So, one can only be, solely just by being,
Actively and simply on side of the I AM.
It is a choice among others.
One is only if one has for himself the One
Who Himself is true life and the way and the truth.
And having Him, one has it all.

Bless The Lord

Bless the Lord, O my soul, come bless His holy name!
Bless the Lord, O my soul, my being, do the same!
Don't forget all His gifts!

He pardons all your sins, He heals your every ill,
Pulls your life from the pit where you'd be dwelling still,
Your soul now chaste and swift,

Fills your days with good things, renewed like the eagle.
The Lord does righteous deeds, with the oppressed, mingles.
The Lord, at all time, bless!

He revealed to Moses and performed mighty deeds,
Merciful and gracious is the good Lord indeed,
Abounding in kindness.

The Lord seldom rebukes, the Lord's slow to anger,
And as your sins merit, He recalls no longer,
From Love and compassion.

As the Heavens tower high up above the earth,
So the great Love of God to his faithful, gives mirth
Way beyond man's reason.

As far as you see east is apart from the west,
So far as all your sins are taken from your chest,
For Love of his children,

He knows how we are formed; remember we are dust.
Like flowers we blossom then quickly die and burst,
Like the field rotten grain.

The Lord's forever kind, faithful from age to age,
Blesses posterity, his covenant as gage,
If his precepts fulfilled,

God's throne is in Heaven and there, rules over all,
He blesses all angels attentive to his call,
Obedient to his will.

Bless the Lord all you hosts, to his will, come attend
And all living creatures, all over God's domain,
Bless the Almighty still!

Veni Creator Spiritus

O come, O come, Holy Spirit,
Come in our hearts and make us whole!
Come and regenerate Thy souls,
Come with Thy flame and make them fit!

Comforter in adversity,
Saving Grace from Heaven's mercy,
Come and attest God's clemency,
Living Source, Fire, Charity!

Come and bestow Thy seven gifts,
Come and promote the Father's Love
Who, from the Heavens, up above,
Renders our ears alert and swift.

Come enlighten our judgment,
Come and restore our willingness.
Come and offset nature's weakness
Befalling all our elements.

Cast far from us the dreaded foe,
Give us the peace the Lord promise'.
That under Thy care we dismiss
The enemy's repeated blows.

Come and teach us to see God's Face
In every life we daily meet.
That we glorify God's Spirit
In daily keeping the Lord's pace.

Glory be to our Lord Jesus!
Glory to the Father on high!
Glory to the Spirit who, by
His precious gifts, makes us pious!

Bestow, O precious God, Thy Holy Spirit upon us
And rekindle the hearts Thou created
And, thus, Thou shall renew the face of the Earth!

Holy God, Mighty God, Immortal God, Thou who instructed the hearts of Thy faithful by the power of Thy Spirit, give us today of this Spirit. That having made us savor and treasure His Goodness, He lavishly grants us the blessed joy of His divine graces, through the same Jesus-Christ, our Lord! Amen!

When They're Gone

The emptiness they live behind,
The vacuum when you cannot find
The loved one for whom you so pine
Is to the mind so disturbing.

The emptiness you fall into
Whenever that dear you know who
Decides to see no more of you,
Cause of your visceral tearing.

You physically feel you're drowning,
Desperately you are air grasping,
Trying to hold to anything
Your shattered world reconciling.

But nothing can come and replace
The voice nor the familiar face
Whose souvenirs you can't erase
And get back to daily living…

The emptiness you left behind
Will so disturb my lonely mind
And put my poor heart in a bind
Of, against these odds, keep beating.

Nothing

Nothing can come close to the thrill,
Nothing, when from your mind you drill.
Nothing, when finally, you feel
The outcome of your creation.

Nothing, when words you don't possess
With pen to paper give caress
And to your eyes in turn impress,
When you face the inspiration.

Nothing compares to the time spent
Nothing, when there, under your tent
You savor the idea content
When mind and muse make connection.

Nothing I say, nothing on Earth
Is more thrilling then to give birth
To the thoughts hidden in her girth;
Essence of her revelation.

From nothing then to blessed some,
My dear I promise I will come
Always to offer your bosom
The bouquet of my emotions.

My Ikigay

Alone when I frantically walk
In the troubling maze of my thoughts,
Reclined yet puzzled and distraught
By all the reason-why's I stalk',
The ones behind all my have-nots.

There, in the mirror of my fate,
I see a man devoid and poor,
Crushed and drowning in the downpour
Of griefs crashing on the estate
Of his world like never before.

I taste the once upon-a-time's.
I feel the hands that slipped away.
I still can hear in my mind's sleigh
The sound of my past Christmas chime
Resonate like it was today.

But in this sadness rising high,
In this, cause of all my torments,
My hopes remain tranquil, dormant,
Not once troubled by the gray sky
Overcasting my firmament.

Upon this sphere where I stifle,
Mourning her hand resting in mine,
The halo of my angel fine
Redirects the care I shuffle,
Going through my long idyll line.

Sure I remain a lone ranger
Searching for the sole companion,
Who'd ward off the false emotion
Lurking whenever a stranger
Come to trip my dedication.

As it's been so long decided,
Any soul has only one mate.
About this there is no debate.
My heart's been steadily guided
By her light glow soft and innate.

Alone therefore I change the tune
And frankly, right out of my vault,
I quickly reach and press default,
To safely land on sandy dune
And hug again my MariJune.

My Junebug

And I love you still
My stifling heart you fill,
Thoughts of you soothe my ills
And I thank God for you

People don't understand
That I can take your hand
By closing my eyes and
Relive our life anew.

But yes, I know
It's on my private screen
That I play all these scenes
And it's feeding my sorrow.

But I won't let
These memories just depart,
They feed my very heart
And it's my only outlet.

But do you love me still,
Is my battle uphill,
Have you long my fate seal'?
I pray God that's not so.

For when I hear your name
My heart still leaps the same
For my spirit you tame…
Like him, I just don't know.

Junedreaming

(Slumberings)

Daydreaming I pull you near
In my tub of lavender,
Truly unable to steer
In or out of my slumber.

In my sleepy thoughtfulness
I fade away silently.
Conversely my consciousness
Will see you or will see me.

Went back to catch up with you
In the land of your sweet dream.
Nothing stays and nothing's true,
All come apart at the seams.

From either side of the bed
Every scene comes shine aglow
And the scent that lies ahead
In my mind resounds hollow.

Tenderly from dusk to dawn
I miss you in my embrace
And I'll be straw on your lawn
Till you breathe life in my face.

Her song

Searching for you right from the start,
Stopping us from being apart
And nothing else matters to me.
Holding you tight against my life,
Dissipating my inner strife,
And all the rest is so petty.

I am the shoulder for your cross,
The toddler child whose mother's lost
In a large crowd at St James fair,
I am the shadow on your wall
Who did not hear the morning call
And stayed caught in this love affair.

I am the fish out of your pond
Who stiffles while you don't respond
To its so desperate gesturing,
I am the sound in your ears
Resounding softly for it fears
To become whisper annoying.

Cherry Love

Close to me so loving
Glide into my arms
With your shadow dancing
Touch me with your charm
For my cherry love
Time is a big tease
For you my betrothed
And the birds and bees.

From the look of all
It doesn't make sense
Listen to my call
Give our love a chance
Open up your pod
Say you love me too
For the love of God
Please let me go through.

Now down on my knees
I long to savor
O my darling please
Let me devour
You can moan and groan
You can call all saints
But there on your throne
Give me your consent.

Right against the norms
And all the taboos
See your brook perform
Pouring your sap through,
I drink your substance
Like a fish stifling
As a recompense
I give you my spring.

And the moon connives
With mounts and valleys,
My pen inner drives
Merge into follies.
Like shivering pups
Under southern sky
The night envelops,
Gives us wings to fly.

Close to me still loving
Glide into my arms
Now shadow whispering
Touch me with your charm
For my Cherry love
From heavens above
Time will always tease
All the birds and bees.

Tween us Two

Tween New York and Connecticut,
Tween a job here and a job there,
Tween a smoothie and a doughnut
My mind curtain suffers a tear
And you appear fresh and uncut.

Tween my short night and my long day,
Tween all the care I so provide,
Tween the times I forget to pray,
I pray mournfully deep inside
For what one day I sent away.

Tween the way home and way to work
Tween the false hopes suffered often,
Tween a thought that my spirit perks
And the rest my spirit dampens
I think of me as a sad jerk.

Tween the wives and the you-know-who's,
Tween the many ones gone too soon,
Tween the ones who remind of you
My heart replays like a cartoon
This love that once was tween us two.

Your Love Song

I will never believe
That others won't receive
None of this legacy
Framed by this secrecy
Of the so many views
Of the bond of us two.
If I should die today
Despite the come what may
I hope my dream come true
To write you a love song.

For you, my darling dear
I wish I could draw near
The perfect choice of words.
So many ones are stirred
Cascading endlessly
Over my mind's valley.
I tried to make them mine
But I could never find
The right set finally
To write you a love song.

*So many the dramas
And pay back of karma
We had to see right through.
Some for me, some for you
But always to enhance
Our wicked romance,
Joining you, joining me
Today we patiently
Pray that our dream come true
And make you a love song.*

*But to nourish the flame
In vain I tried to tame
This semantic downpour.
I shout like none before
But the crowd on my path
Though they try not to laugh
Will always veer to me
When they hear that I spree
The love I have for you,
Cause of this, your love song.*

You Again

Here you are in my arms again
Steady as a summer refrain,
Lovely and cheery like the fall.
Here you are in my world anew,
My clouds your sunshine pierced right through,
You must have heard my silent call.

Here you are in my arms again
My composure I can't regain
Bathing in the bright of your smile.
You returned to take possession
And my sorrows make concession
Of what they claimed for a long while.

Here you are again in my arms.
Succumbing to your jolly charms
Nothing can be ever sweeter.
Sweaty palms and palpating heart
Pierced again by your subtle dart
And your face ever more cuter.

Oh damn you! Right into my life
You come to settle any strife
That might have rattled my status
Of lonely dude ever kissing
The lips that so long been missing
To which he held on mordicus.

Here you are, here you are, but how
Did you realize that the vow
I made not to date was serious?
It's just that always when in cage
The heart ignores any visage
Different from that of its Precious.

Here you are and what a pleasure
That you still remember Roger;
He wouldn't have stopped wagging its tail.
He took it harder your absence,
He suffered, suffered in silence
Even causing its heart to fail.

But here you are inquiring;
No flowers at your welcoming.
There were none in my icy land.
The rare buds in my entourage
Were sadly always a mirage
And the sun was never at hand.

But here right in my life again
You come back your throne to regain,
Victorious queen of lonely heart,
Now that you replanted your flag
To the whole world you can go brag
But from me please never depart.

NYC Farewell

And now that all is said and done,
Of old grudges I carry none.
Wounded in the battles I won,
I'll take a final bow.

Faithful have been the companions,
The ones who helped me carry on
Facing the many deceptions
That I suffered somehow.

Many have been the dilemmas,
Scouring have been all the traumas
Reaped from the transcending karmas
To instill the lessons.

But in this well-deserved furlough
I choose to size my highs and lows
And to my so wounded fellows
I'm still begging pardon.

For this ride home can be brutal
And though the blows were not fatal
They were far from being festal,
Hurting down to the bone.

Like life, love promises nothing
But to fill your heart with feelings,
Source of most of your sufferings;
Wisdom written in stone.

But now that all has been declared,
Now that the chosen have been paired
And the innocents have been spared,
I slowly take my load

And bid farewell to my loved ones,
Those who stood for me more than once
And this troubled city renounce
To head for my abode.

Morning Stillness

In the stillness of the morning,
Lord Jesus, come abide in my soul,
Be my companion in all things,
You, my trembling heart yearns to behold.
Aren't You the truest of friend,
Whose sweet remembrance keeps me awake
While my night draws near to its end
And my spirit its night stroll, still takes.

Just like to Your humble plower
Steady the plow in every row,
Guide my footsteps, O dear Savior,
Upon the ground where nothing yet grows,
So that my plowshare can dig deep,
Your divine strength put deep within me
So that good harvest I can reap
And I voice not any blasphemy.

To win over non-believers,
Poor sinners that the world still ensnares,
Deep in my heart put the fever,
That love is stronger when it is shared,
If the hurdles are too many,
If the enemy comes in my way
That instead of fear, if any,
You come and dispel the doubt away.

If I grow tired and weary,
Have pity, Lord, for my trembling hand,
Come to me, please, in a hurry,
Together we will finish the land,
Remain with me until nightfall
And when time will come to take my rest
Closer to You my head will fall
And You will safeguard my humble nest.

In God we trust

From the very first shades of this life given dawn,
From the early babble that we tenderly spawn,
Cradled by mother's care,
From all the sounds that lend and come to shape the mind,
From jolly airs that sing this love that we come find,
From parents' cuddling stare,

From the spring that we sprang, jovial, running, playing,
From the first of sad blows that deep in the heart, rings,
Spreading bouts of sadness
The promising echo of God's great Love for us,
Instilled fresh in our hearts by mentors so pious,
With love and tenderness,

The love of God has been, through the joy or the mess,
Through the many downfalls that we fail to confess,
Subtle and yet steady,
The force all-powerful, the hand ever present
That always dries the tears once He hears we repent
From all, to remedy.

Then we come simmering, right in our life summer
And all that we were taught seem to make us dumber,
In societal trend,
And we feel to adjust we have to, like in Rome,
Do what pleases the crowd to fit under the dome,
And the Spirit, offend.

We create our own laws, reshuffling the standards
That, from the time of old, have brought us the rewards
Of God's blessed children
We fill up our misses and smother our conscience,
That deep within the soul, receives every grievance,
Sent by other brethren.

But God's love still remains, all through the loads of pain,
Through the mounts and valleys that the landscapes contain,
Patiently He follows
And still keeps on the talk that we choose to ignore,
Go on perpetrating, just like dreaded encores:
The roots of our sorrow.

Then we fall in the fall and slowly reconvene,
All over life, scattered, the bits of what we've been,
On the trail, self trampled,
And try to reconstruct, surfing our own distress,
Resulting of the blows given in wickedness
To the self we tumble.

For then as our blue sky changes to golden tint,
Points at our horizon the slew of the complaints
That we now inherit,
Coming to our senses, still blessed in the mire,
We recollect the laws we once had admired,
To ease our spirit.

Still there, the Love of God, steady in His embrace,
Gives us the momentum to come finish the race
And perform the repair
Much needed to sustain the graces once bestow',
Those we feverishly try to find from below
The rubbles we once bear.

In winter, when we win, for having dwelt safely,
Under building graces that the Father only
Can sustain in our hearts,
We come as true winners, all filled with the richness,
Those He had once promised, once His Spirit we bless
And to others impart.

Or when the week mind fails, acting its disregard,
When we don't recognize that look vague and haggard,
Demented, forgetful,
When we rely on care, in every day living,
From concerned relatives, so worried and hurting,
Facing the pitiful

Then ready, unburdened, reflecting His great Love,
Peacefully we set up our eyes on up above,
Devoid of earthly lust,
For then we know for sure that we have done our best
And though throughout the years we failed so many tests,
Truly, in God we trust'.

Deep Inside

There must be deep inside the most common of us
A subtle connection with the great non-obvious.
Always a voice is heard from deep within the chest
Reminding us the way to reach our treasure nest.

The soul treading the Earth, in its lenghty journey,
Often vaguely recalls the well-taught litanies
That the spirit, the life, the light, the sustainer,
Uses all day, all night, its Maker to honor.

The dialogue exists, non-ending, all life through,
And all the directives are given clear and true.
They are sent to enlight, sent as most needed food,
Keeping the sojourner in best spiritual mood.

Thus this treasure dwells in unheard of by the most
But when the link's severed, the common sense is lost.
For when all light's out darkness slowly pervades.
You don't know left from right, virtue ethics evade,

And what's left is a mind torn amid dilemmas,
Unable to discern and steer from miasma.
It is led to its doom all so maliciously
Like a blind on a leash across a mine valley.

See, all throughout the world, down from its foundation
Good and evil battle to grasp generations.
All through the centuries, since the dawning of time,
Humans are caught between somber knell and bright chime.

This notion is conveyed from fathers down to sons.
If assimilated it wards off curse thereon.
But nowadays the line, once clear demarcation,
Has slowly disappeared, causing no reaction

For the world has lost all senses of direction.
From deep inside nothing is heard, no transmisssion.
The spirit within us by iniquities quelled,
No longer can be heard. So nothing it can tell.

And so around the world come surface brand new gods,
And what they say is gold though infantile and odd.
They are revered as such, as ones to follow now,
And large crowds deep in awe to all they say just bow.

But deep inside despite this non-ending vacarme
From all the Earth corners rings aloud the alarm
Calling the lost brethren back to their Creator,
Of all things the Maker, of all lives the Author.

The hardening of hearts that we've been warned about
Now is perpetrated and belched at every shout.
Loudly they want freedom, loudly they want severed,
From the Vigne they belong, the ties of forever.

And the order of things topsy-turvy becomes.
Virtue gates are opened, every vice finds a home.
And we see cavalcade strings of calamities.
The world karma is soiled by varied enmities.

The spirit resilience comes straight from its Maker.
It gives life and sustains. Of all blows the taker.
But in the re-entry where all books are opened,
Every ounce of offense is dealt with right and then.

But deep within the core, meanwhile under the blows,
The spirit makes amend, pleads for us here below.
It sends out loud sighs but remains as planted
In its decadent host, as guest ever slighted.

And days in and days out, it carries its burden.
It sustains every life and bears crosses often.
Like its divine Maker it takes all silently,
Offenses of all kinds thrown deliberately.

But it would be wise to nurture
Since it gives life to our nature
From the first heartbeat.
It is of life the true essence,
The sole cause of our resilience,
Safe of divine treats.

And since it supports every growth,
Sheer destruction it truly loathes,
The rebel's favorite,
When it's given rightful honor,
It's permeates our demeanor,
Making us complete.

It carries us through centuries,
Helps us every burden carry,
All under God's eye,
Nothing escapes this inner scope,
It catches every time we mope,
Every time we cry.

But then we go daily shunning
This the true light, source of our being
Bluntly unaware,
That this light given us, sustains.
It's the life we live that maintains,
Making us God's heirs.

But always deep inside, from where life animates,
Lies in somber secret the meaning of it all:
That we should always be at God's beckons and call,
That giving of ourselves surely betters our fate.

For often deep inside we decide otherwise,
The world and its demands smother the little voice.
And the rebel watching finds reason to rejoice
Since once again we fail to gain a better prize.

When a chance is offered, as always in our life,
We hope that we're ready to respond and strike gold.
For if serving the Lord the true Christian upholds,
Of nothing but blessings one then becomes so rife.

The serving of the Lord brings about His Kingdom.
Then in turn He blesses well packed down on one's lap.
Then down generations it trickles, never flops,
Offering golden pearls right from Heavens bosom.

Tales of great encounters are narrated often
Where deep within their hearts they felt so much compelled.
For when the Lord beckons, every doubt is dispelled.
A lighthearted reply is fitted to obtain.

But such a scenario is often not the case.
While making a living we just chose to ignore
The voice always so clear that deep within the core,
Reveals the Lord's mandate the mind chooses to chase.

Then we go our own way smothering the candle
Since with our agendas it would overtly clash.
We quickly find excuse or just silently smash
The deep invitation we deem we can't handle.

But the Lord goes around and again and again
Comes and knocks at the door, expecting a "fiat".
But each and every time the answer rings just flat,
Much afraid of losing what thus far we have gained.

The day you hear His voice, do not harden your heart,
For He comes to give you a shot at His Kingdom
That you, day after day, ought to seek as outcome,
In order to one day , see His heaven's rampart.

Therefore from deep within, this source of emission,
Surges more than often the voice dwelling in us.
Woe to whosoever remains oblivious,
He'd be slowly working at his soul perdition.

More than often in this here life,
More than often of gains so rife,
More than often we loose all tracks
Of the true meaning of living,
So lost in this poor world blingbling
That we just can't find the way back.

The bleak irony in this case
Is that once depleted of grace,
Lost is the sense of direction.
Then the soul of this unaware
Strives but quickly heads to nowhere,
Rendered deaf by our volition.

The Guide is always there speaking.
The Shepperd leads all His earthling,
Back to where they always belong.
But the rebel always comes spoil
What Heavens has so longer toiled,
Causing misery all life long.

But deep inside, repeatedly,
Voices ring out so pressingly
Trying to avert miseries
But we remain on the pit course,
The one of every grief the source,
Cause of all types of penuries.

One truly lives a bleak nightmare,
Walking around with empty stare
When the soul's not quenched by its Source.
All that's given should be received
Or else solace one can't retreive
Thus pants upon its journey course.

Whereas when enlighted one lives
A purposeful life and so breathes
And radiates love all around.
It is seen in every gesture
And heard in all that one utters
That one's fed from where love abounds.

There the soul in utmost delight
Lives and exists bathing in light.
Actions are clean and lighthearted.
All thoughts are clear, beaming outward
To the welfare of the vineyard.
One's future is hence safeguarded.

For as one gives so one receives.
Every branch cares for its own leaves
Thus wellfare for all is obtained.
Care of neighbor is then ensured.
And no toil alone is endured
Thus love among us all remains.

Therefore we realize how lovely life can be.
We live in harmony, as God's heirs wannabe.
For deep inside us all the Love of the Master
Sustains life within us, makes our hearts beat faster.

And good old creation goes back to its dawning
And nature gleams of joy, the world karma's shinning.
And charity prevails for in all hearts there's love,
All that breathes trustfully leans on the God above.

Deep inside all is heard and gladly resonate.
Peace all around pervades and so love emanates.
And all of His childern receive their basic due
For all around the world God spreads His bléssed dew.

No more war, sin is quelled. All rebels sent away.
The Earth remains on course, her seasons find their sway,
And the sea to her shores tales what's hidden thus far. Sunrays are
more golden sending love to each star.

And thus the Word of God, dwelling in every heart
Would enhance creation down to its hidden parts.
And the world would live on under the divine watch
For truly deep inside, all that He says we'd catch.

Eventual emergence

When tomorrow will dawn
At the end of our days,
When all is said and done,
With nothing more to say,
Drowning in bitter gall,

When the sun will dangle
Like a meek ball of fire,
When stars will fall, mingle,
Heading to retire
To some celestial pall,

When the thunder so loud
Will waken dead corpses,
When the heaviest clouds
Will trade in their stances,
Flattened when once so tall,

When every uttered truths
Will come knock at all doors,
When cheap talk no more smoothe
With their petty downpour
To cath Earth in her fall

Then we'll stand, well aware,
That every Word was true.
Then we'll stand and just stare
At this Kingdom brand new

Now exposed in plain sight
For those who would not see,
For those too scared to fight
The vile insurgency.

Then they'll stand and take in
The Awesomeness at hand
While feeling the pouring
Of bitter gall extend.

At these unsettled times, to say the least of much,
Times when all blasphemies will finally find a hush,
Times when all the faithful, with hearts bursting of joy,
Will be set up apart, safe from the wrath deployed,

We will stand and witness the Might of the Maker,
Who by His mighty Hand have kept all stars in place.
And basking in the bliss whose faith was the baker
We'll take our place swiftly in God's peaceful palace.

But until this D day that no one seems to fear,
Until these dark hours closing all our eras,
We'll face the bitterness growing wild around here
And suffer in the core the wicked ones aura

Which would cripple the world, and life as we know it.
Whatever we invest will be paid at that time
For the soul has it all, all failures, all merits,
All that to the brethren we gave as care or crime.

Oh! That we should invest for these foreseen hours!
That we should plan ahead even if in deep doubt!
For if what-if's remain and our mind devour,
Humbly ask for some faith that gives much needed clout.

And while at it, just pray. Pray that the Lord's goodness,
In His mighty power make you strong and able.
For the rebel will come, knowing well your weakness,
To trip your every step, snare you with his cables.

For his role is always to offer you detours,
And quick resolutions to every desire.
Do not be fooled, I say, don't even take a tour
Of wealth he will display to entice your fire.

Ignoring the standing will not declare you safe.
Ignoring the standing, they get to snap you in.
Ignoring the standing will get you to be strafed
For your only true shield sadly was not built in.

You carry it in you this shield, throughout your life,
Daily living for Him, daily doing His chores.
A world of God's children of miseries are so rife
Take care of those you can, carry them in your core.

For since you do to Him as to the least of them,
The Lord will in return your every step secure.
And deep within your heart your love for Him will stem,
And He will be your shield, guard you without failure.

In this non-ending war generating your strife,
Never truce is given, stands out no neutral ground.
Daily you must attest, choosing love, choosing life,
Choosing to serve your God now that He can be found.

In the midst of all these keep your eyes on the prize,
And before you know it your time will be at hand.
The Lord in everything will keep on you His eyes
Leading you but safely back to the promised land.

Said and done

There, after all is said and done,
After all stamina is gone
From the body,
After all the cheap talk is sown,
And of nonsense there'll be left none
To parody,

When the spirit will now emerge
Unclutered by the body surge
Of ego trip,
When dear wisdom will deem it wise
To come and witness the demise
Of pride so deep,

When we'll face up with nothing left
But the real richness that has leapt
Free of decay,
When we recall childhood treasures,
Real essence of our true nature,
Once tucked away,

If blessèd we'll go rekindle
The flame of our first old candle,
Leading beacon,
To return not against our will
To the mighty Source where love spills,
Where truth beckons.

Gladly we'll then go reconnect
And give honor, praise and respect
To God above,
And with contrite, sorrowful heart,
Lightly we'll await to depart
Where resides Love.

Ask and receive

The creature dwelling in nature
Was given right on its treasures
To use as it sees fit.
He comes and rightfully plunders,
And all good things puts asunder,
Trampled down with its feet.

So the richness of the whole world,
Precious metals, diamonds and pearls
All scooped by just a few,
Created what we witnesss now
As a crisis that has somehow
Reached every mind purview.

But the loving Father concerned,
He who needs and desires discerns,
Made it so that we still,
Through faithful prayers we come ask
And patiently leave Him the task
To give His flock their fill.

So come and ask for every grain,
No matter how you feel you're drained
Humbly wait till He gives
Much needed seeds to grow your crop
For His wisdom is way on top
Of what your mind conceives.

For there, the secret of this life
Is knowing that in every strife
The Lord comes to our aid,
And by asking we develop
This climate where God envelops
Us since for this we're made.

Blind Faith

I trust in You, O Lord, truly I trust in You.
I trust in You but it's because You want me to.
When alone with my mind I reach and come to You
It's because You beckon. Right there I follow through.

Who am I, O my Lord, that makes You reach for me
And then make germinate all this love within me.
It pulls me at all times to come and draw from You
All that is good and pure, all that is clean and true.

All along my journey I keep my hand in yours
Knowing ever surely the tricks of its decors.
But trustingly I go, while to safety You lead,
Living the life You preach, free of pride, free of greed.

But always, my dear Lord, always, and this I know,
Always in my weakness I miss my tomorrrow,
The plans You have for me to grow and to prosper
Always they get trampled by the beast, the ripper.

But You relentlessly restock my heritage
And always You manage to free me from bondage.
I trust in You, O Lord, really I trust in You
For always You provide for me a slate brand new.

Praise to YOU

From the dawning of time till this day that You nest,
Your Spirit's been with us and never took a rest.
It renders all fecund so to grow and prosper
Through the life that You give, and of love the reaper.

Through eras, centuries, the years and the seasons
Your Love for us resounds baffling every reason.
It's reflected daily through the Earth You secure
Keeping her on her track during her every tour.

For the Earth, O dear God, if we're ever to've known,
Faces at every stance a fate so uncommon,
A demise that no one whthin their foggy mind,
If ever thought about, could've ever defined.

The Earth around the sun, runs a circuit oblong,
On a most steady path, and it's been for so long.
Has anyone wonder whatever would happen
If one day our sweet Earth would fall in some deep end?

The deep end of spinning around, without control,
The deep end of failing to care for us poor souls...
This planet where our God once trod and has His heirs,
This planet would not stand without His steady care.

For the Lord loves the Earth for there He put His brood.
There He chose to rear them, give them their daily food,
There with His archangels, leads it through all epochs,
That's where the big rebel chose to wreak his havoc.

Now we can all deduct that countries in turmoil
Are by far the few ones with the most blessed soil.
They endure the unrest and all of the above
Just because they're chosen to receive God's most love.

The Earth therfore remains in the palm of His hand.
She's cradled lovingly will not reach the deep end.
Her Father's archangels monitor all her moves,
Hence her steady circuits Her God's steady Love proves.

And she gladly gyrates through every known eras
As she spins on herself to warm every aura.
All done at a distance to give us the right warmth
To nurture every life, be it on land or wharf.

Praise be to God above who with His steady care
Minds the course of the Earth, spinning her fair and square.
Through careful archangels He keeps her on her track,
Under their watchful eyes He knows she'll never slack.

Tomorrow

When alone one ponders over what lies ahead,
The silent that echoes comes back dreary and bleak.
The muted tomorrow to no one ever sheds
A hint, a peep, a sound, nothing rolls down its beak.

The great unknown lies bare with vast, hidden valleys
From where all things trickle silently and unseen
To the wise, the sane ones and those off their trollies,
The saints, the not so bad and those profoundly mean,

Every one will receive their rightful comeuppance.
The universe is set to return silently
Whatsoever one throws back to its provenance.
Humans tend to devise their fate diligently.

No one ever listens to the shouts loud and clear,
Warning us night and day of all looming dangers.
No one ever prospects how it can be so near,
Thinking that requital befalls only strangers.

Repugnant is the flow running down every street,
The stench is now welcome, upheld and sought after.
It's taught in every school, in high places have seats
But leads to once foretold, widely spread disasters

Which are the goal pursued, the desired chaos.
For the instigator, the author of the mess
Wants everyone edgy, unsettled and just lost
Devoid of common sense, gift of Creator blest.

Tomorrow will appear for us as day of doom
For we day after day bear the new scenery.
We seem not to fathom that on us darkness looms
For we cater weakly to widespread treachery.

And at every sunrise we miss the precious goal
And drift further, further from the Source of all Light.
The truth that was uttered, needed re-entry toll,
We'll be lacking it all at the pearly gate site.

And tomorrow will stand quiet, cold and placid
Watching us get buried under one's own grievance.
We won't believe how duped, all now rendered lucid,
We have been for so long from widespread connivance.

So stoically we'll stand facing the come-what-may,
Unaware of the time, the day nor the hour
But for sure tomorrow, bearer of sunny days,
Will never fail on us to unveil its power.

Divine Patience

But I want the whole world to know
That on this earth God runs the show.
What He allows He has foretold
In solemn speech uttered so bold.

Then to allow His Father's will
To perform as a rod of steel
And bring about blesséd Kingdom
To the much displeasing of some

HE let the proud have the conceit
That the whole world is at their feet,
All over, hither and thither,
They spread miseries thereafter.

HE sees the wars with bloody ground,
HE sees all disasters abound.
HE sees the frown of His children,
Their cries rising as sad refrain.

All is taken into account.
All that spiritually amount
To either side of His justice,
Catering hell or seeking bliss.

There again the choice is given
To help the dove or be raven,
Outcome that always sets the stage
To be winner or fall hostage.

This choice is ours while we're alive,
Helping through dilemmas and strives.
It sheds light on thoughts and actions,
Simmering down all emotions.

The final hour will ring one day,
The final hour never delays,
The final hour will chase away
All trace of pride, all shades of grey

That once upon covered the Truth
That was uttered from divine Mouth
To give us strength for the journey
Done then under sin tyranny.

As it did in the days of old
His patience that for us unfolds
Stands there taking every affront
Done unto Him, Love divine Font.

At my horizon

The Lord is good in all His ways,
Cares for us all throughout our days,
Of this we are sure,
In subtle ways He leads His flock
Through it all, steady as a rock
In all they endure.

Nothing can escape His spirit,
This life, safekeeper of all treats,
Display of His might.
There He infuses all notions,
There He suffers all our actions
He sees clear and bright.

The very least of desires,
The ones setting up our fires
Deep with the heart,
Are scoped by His all-loving Eye.
Not one to Him is ever sly,
From their very start.

But through all the thick and the thin,
He minds the life He puts within,
The spirit in us.
He judges every desire,
Steadily and never tires,
So insiduous.

They have to align with His plan,
His plan to tread His divine land,
In a safe return,
They have to promote His kingdom
They should not offend His wisdom
As for them we yearn.

But in His almighty science
He grants us as true indulgence
Our soul desires,
And often He puts them instead,
Deep in the heart where they are fed
To bring us higher.

The desires we hold so dear,
That last thoughout the many years
Are the blessèd ones,
The ones branded of divine stamp,
The ones the Heavens really vamp,
Stand equal to none.
Therefore the Lord in His goodness
Will favor and secretly bless
The deepest yearnings,
For there He teaches us patience
Along blessèd perseverance,
In silent sufferings.

The Lord thus bestows His blessings,
And every treasure to us brings
As soon He sees fit.
And whatever is His promise
To secretly the soul appease
Goes through our spirit.

For the dear Lord in his goodness
Always chooses His flock to bless
Based on their merit,
And always, always He rewards
Show of perseverance towards
His mighty Spirit.

His Words are light, life and guidance,
His Words incite perseverance
In the faithful heart,
Which keeps them deep within its core,
Chews on them encore and encore,
Cherishing all parts.

They till their soil and bring about
The Lord's kingdom in all that sprout
Sharing His graces.
They bring them joy, bring them solace,
On the journey, help them keep pace
As the foe chases.

Then He, the giver of good gift,
In return, plentiful and swift,
Gives us His rewards,
For the Lord is faithful and true,
His promises all bring their dues
To faithful stewards.

But as for me I'll always dwell,
Steadfast till from within His well
My Lord grants my wish.
He promised so in Him I hope
Knowing well He helps me to cope,
Missing the cherished.

But one day at my horizon,
During my most cherished season
A clear day of fall,
For standing firm in His Promise
I will receive the one I miss,
Not delayed at all.

Castaway

After much rigorous swimming
Finally we reached this small isle
Peaceful, green with dune welcoming
Souls like us to rest for a while.

We tried so hard not to anchor
But when in life you're castaway
You pick the whatever décor
That the good Lord puts on your way.

So now that some precious solace
Was sent to us bearing much care,
That the weary look of our face
Would be just erased fair and square.

After much rigorous swimming
Then releived, we'll lay ourselves down
And caressed by the breeze blowing
We'll blot out one another's frown.

No one will ever come disturb
The tender moments of embrace.
No one since we'll need not to curb
The loving glance glowing our face.

The echo of our escapade
Will never reach their prying ears.
No eavesdroper will try to raid
On sweet nothings said with no fear.

The blue waters with foamy waves
Will always come and bring the news
Of this old world lost and depraved
For which we were so much enthused.

The fauna of exotic birds
Seems to want to show us the way
As they repeatedly throw words
Upon tree branches as they sway.

The sun daily brings its blessings,
The dawn, so I can see your eyes,
That shine your love right from their screen,
Your face, where my fate meets her size.

And we spend days, and we spend nights
Cloistered in this eden so fair,
Never leaving each other's sight,
Living as the most blessèd pair.

As dawn comes chase away the stars,
As the moon loses its splendor,
As the dew by the sun gets charred
The isle displays all its candor.

Amidst it all, you shine the best,
You portray a cute peachy doll.
I must have aced some serious test
To be winner in such a poll.

Spending time in your entourage,
Cuddle and then cuddle encore
Turn into bliss this island cage
Where we give it all from the core.

Long gone the sad ending of days
When we'd part from one another.
Long gone that dark gloom that would lay
Your absence, my heart to smother.

After much vigorous swimming
We give thanks for this joyous fate,
For in this most fortunate swing
Life gave us a non-ending date.

"Since I Have Now Savored…"

Since I have now savored from your cup full to date,
Since in your loving hands, rested my weary head,
Since at times I drew in, soft and affectionate,
Of your soul the essence, as the end of day treads,

Since I have been blesséd as you whisper to me
These gilded words of love sprinkled with tenderness,
Since with laughter or tears, happy or just gloomy,
Your lips have touched my lips, for my eyes to witness,

Since to my sheer delight I have gazed on the shine
Of your candid aura, alas, lightly shaded,
Since I've seen the tumble in my life, this deep brine,
Of a rose petal fall, as from your life faded,

Now I can calmly say to these fast rolling years:
Go, go and keep strolling! I can slowly grow old,
Go on as you do best, as your fallen leaves veer,
An eternal flower has bloomed deep in my soul!

Nothing will come trouble, as you shuffle about,
The chalice I indulged and that in turn I filled.
My soul is now richer than your calender clout!
My heart is now fonder than your time could have spilled!

Daily retreat

Watching you leave disrupts my flow of jolly thoughts,
Watching you leave unearths all my childhood nightmares,
Watching you leave comes free all the sadness once caught
That then ran down freely in my soul rendered bare.

Watching you leave resounds deep in the heart of mine
To dismantle the peace that from your eyes I stole.
Watching you leave offers only prongs and pure brine
To the thirst I cradle deep in my stricken soul.

Watching you leave comes and tremples my sanity,
Watching you leave awakes the remnants of my fear,
Watching you leave trashes all instilled clarity
With which my heart follows your heart upon this sphere.

Watching you leave comes drench my given inner drive
And leaves me deep rooted in mire of distress,
Watching you leave insults and right there it deprives
Of all sense of goodness, of treasured cheerfulness.

Watching you leave impales the inner desire
To spend my every day in realm of your shadow,
And so watching you leave will smother the fire
That now burns in my heart since you first said hello.

Shady Glow

On this quiescent foggy dawn,
Deep in this smothered misty morn,
From the dim light the sun could spawn
Surges a day from sadness born.

It peeps over Mother Nature,
Of the right time so unaware.
What it delivers is for sure
The best shade of light it can spare.

It glides over plains and valleys,
Over leaves and over roses.
It bathes nettles and bathes hollies
With the fresh dew it proposes.

It strives alone without sunrays
Sprinkling its gloom so evenly
But spreads its moisture all the way,
Quenching all buds ever gently.

The melancholy it unfurls
Over hearts and souls wreak havoc,
Even the pretty made up girls
See flattened down their curls and locks.

No beak to voice the least of cheep,
For birds dwell softly in their nest,
Warm beverages everyone sips
From fear of cold feel in the chest.

A homey feeling hangs around
From lack of conveyed energy,
Since the sunrays don't touch the ground,
With us they form no synergy.

And the clouds linger and tarry,
As on doomsday, swollen and dark.
They muffle and even bury
Kids' voice you could hear in the park.

And the day treads ever slowly
As though not knowing where to go,
Seemingly hoping that swiftly
The sun would pierce for a last show.

And so on such a foggy dawn,
That sees smothered a misty morn,
Any light the good sun could spawn
Comes and cradles all sadness born.

Forbidden Treats

Go tell the spring not to spread out
This warm feeling within the chests.
Remind her to prolong the drought
For none of us deserves her best.

She stealthily brings revival
Deep from Mother Nature bosom.
It permeates as survival
And this all living cells fathom.

Remind the summer to elope.
There's nothing for him to warm here.
Long, long ago faded all hope
Upon this land to see it clear

That the source of all life remains
The One who created it all.
He set them as women and men
For them to heed His every call.

As for autumn she should never
Spread her colors upon the land.
In her advent she should waver
And just cancel all she had planned.

Her indian summer that nurtures,
The shades of her leaves that marvels,
Her soft sunrays gilding nature,
This world stance she won't unravel.

But old winter he can linger,
Run up mountains and down valleys,
Tighten all his frigid fingers
So their cold heart they come tally.

Never has it been shuch a brood,
Scanning down the generations,
Never has it been one that stood
As daring midst all creations.

Mother Nature has been forewarned
And her offspring heeds to her call,
She is to close her every barn
And cast them out of her recall.

Only one season they will have
To dally deep in their mire.
The demerits on their behalf
To their world will set the fire.

Summer love

And when the summer days are gone,
All heading for some distant shore,
When with them taking all the fun,
They'll leave us begging for some more,
More of the love we did partake
In this tender short-lived idyll,
We stand alone amidst heartache
As all around seems to idle.

And when the summer days are gone,
Deep within me I hold you tight.
In your eyes where tenderness shone
All of your promises alight.
But my heart drowning in sadness
Ring all the sunny tunes of love,
The ones we shared with happiness
That with the fallen leaves are shoved.

And when the summer days are gone
We'll hang on tight to souvenirs.
They will ring but will bring us none
But empty dunes those far or near
That witnessed all our escapades
Under the rays with sunny glare,
When with embrace and accolades
To tell you of my love I dared.

And when the summer days are gone,
Leaving empty our hands and arms,
We'll see all affairs come undone
Despite the sway of our young charm.
The promises of teenage years
Like empty shells remain hollow,
They stemmed from innocence and fears,
But melted in wax of sorrow.

And when the summer days are gone,
For they fly from shelves of kindness,
Along with them, all that was sown
Is seen trampled by sheer sadness.
They know well they will soon return,
Three hundred sixty-five more days,
But the feelings the souls now churn
For we're to go our separate ways.

Now that the summer days are gone,
Leaving it all to fall madness,
That comes stir hearts and tries to clone
Other love, other tenderness,
But since they lack the salty sand
They bring but soothing illusion,
That keeps busy our empty hands
Till comes next summer vacation.

Love Poems

I started writing to you my love poems,
You had suddenly emerged and become
By far the precious and forbidden theme
That my mind and soul subtly overcome.

I started writing to you my love poems
Not reallly knowing the end of their game.
You see, you remain on my mind aflamed.
The delight it gained has not seen such high.

I started writing to you my love poems
Because if I don't then, my mind goes lame.
It grew accustomed to your gentle touch,
So far has never indulged under such.

I started writing to you my love poems
Because I can dare reveal soul to soul,
Tender and stealthy, the nature of snare,
You have over mine, in this love affair.

I started writing to you my love poems
Because hand in hand we can walk the aisle
Of this treasured land, belovéd eden,
Uncluttered by sneer, envy and disdain.

I started writing to you my love poems,
For really enthroned on my nervous heart,
Everything you say is golden and true,
Everything you do makes my world brand new.

I started writing to you my love poems
For they subtly come soothe my troubled mind.
Nothing more perturbs when in life you find
Someone to belong but belongs instead.

I started to write to you my love poems.
They all come dwindling to a simple truth
That on my journey you were sent to soothe
The rise and setting of my dreary days.

To your loving eyes I'll write my love poems,
They'll come on their knees and beg you, my love,
Not to be afraid of all the above.
They're just expressions of a lonely heart,

That deep from its sleep dreamed of a fair queen
Who, for goodness sake, and to its surprise,
Had your precious smile and your lovely eyes.
Now it refuses to leave this sweet scene.

Promise

Deep in my mental state
Where fiercely I debate
Over our distant fate
I can see
That never will we do
Cuddle like lovers who
Feel love sincere and true
Ardency.

I sit and take a toll
Of this feeling I hold
Under surest control
To this day
That'd bloomed into the best
Of ever stifling zest
Carried by any chest,
As they say.

For deep within my heart,
Tamed by you from the start,
Your all so-subtle dart
Remains still
And causes day by day
Its throbbing and its sway
To come and dwell your way
For its fill.

You bring it steadily,
Smile yet so lovingly
But hover so rarely
That, it aches.
It wishes you remain
And makes that its domain
Could be yours loud and plain
At all stakes.

Time and all its minutes
Just fly when you're in it
And highlight my defeat
Every day,
I long to be the one
You decide to count on,
Right now and from now on,
Come what may.

As problems come and pile,
And on my mind defile,
Life's always worth its while
Around you.
So that's why I utter
Amidst beats and flutter,
I always thereafter
Will love you.

Devotion

To God I give all thanks, He whose life I carry!
Life is a precious gift; and through it God bestows
Blessings galore and thus Heavens humans marry,
Spreading all gifts on us below.
To every rose offered we get thorns of all size,
And as they age before their eyes,
Humans gladly accept their pain,
And rave for sunny days, as well as for fresh air.
I give all thanks to God, for life lived just and fair
That results to death not in vain!

Unfortunate the man who dies sad and alone
Without passing the torch for a brethren to live,
Without passing to them the baton dear and honed,
So lovingly, before they leave!
Wretched are the people, bearing under a curse,
Panting under the bane they nurse,
Who watch die their name and their pride,
As the whole world ignores or even mourn their fate,
With no dear souvenir left over to relate,
As beacon at their coffin side.

When worn out by our sins, God his wrath unleashes,
He allows disaster on lands to wreak havoc.
And over centuries hideous scar furnishes,
That rests on minds for long epoch.
From just one nasty germ by folks long forgotten
A giant plague rises, rotten,
Spreads its shadow over them all.
The lands try to fence off, but the deadly nuisance,
Like a horrible mate, reaffirming its stance,
Embraces them in a last fall.

Right then crowd of people, under the pestilence,
Fall all over the place, like snow flakes in meadows.
They succumb everywhere and death in its advance
Causes casualties in long rows.
The monster, one by one, its victims comes ensnare,
So they breathe their last breath of air.
Then it feeds off their corpse lifeless
And amidst the pyres, the rubbles and the wakes
The living shelterless, as you flee deadly snakes,
Wander far from corpses graveless.

When the circus opened, those days of funeral,
Romans in time of peace, by their lictor shadowed,
Witnessed then from afar, the victims as they'd fall
Preys of the desert tigers' blows.
So the trembling nations among themselves gathered,
Bawled to the Heavens together,
Their cry from sea to sea carried.
The world in arms fearing the hydra rapid wings,
Keeps right under their scourge all these lifeless beings,
Threatening in dread much hurried.

You city bon vivants, tell me, isn't it true,
That parties are more fun, and pleasures are sweeter,
When it's a worse-off curse than hatred can push through,
That is on sides of fence thither?
Far from blazing layers by dreadful bug sullied,
That worldwide children charmingly,
In loving arms would fall asleep!
That we treasure by far the fresh air of the town,
When nations in mourning, begrudging us with frown,
Afar breathe stench as corpses sip!

Everyone is absorbed by his short-lived circle.
A mother embraces her cuddling young infant
With no notion of where a breast turning purple,
Might kill a child in an instant!
Some cheap pity resounds deep within throbbing hearts,
Between gatherings they took part
And those they'll attend tomorrow,
For to most of humans, mourning is pestering.
They'd gladly shy away from painful gatherings,
Not to meddle in some sorrow.

Then again for others moved by a deep yearning,
They emerge from the crowd, and from each other eyes
Search for some worthy fate, that tomorrow may bring
Upon them some lovely surprise.
A triumphant future hangs bright in their balance?
What hope they lovingly romance?
What gold? What treasure? What honor?
Alas! So it appears in a world so barren
When righteousness is shown on such unkind terrain,
It's seen as happy demeanor.

But folks, these human beings, as led by the Spirit,
Fearlessly face the plague with such a winsome stare.
They charge where the big crowd would never get merit.
Heartily pray for their welfare!
As for you, their parents, their spouses, their mothers,
Your bitter sorrow, please smother.
Allow that the willful victims
Go free from the burden of your reckless wailing
Should they prefer the plague as ultimate sailing,
To those they hold in some esteem?

But soon they step into the so-deserted land.
A horde of living deads call onto them in tears,
Amazed that still on earth, someone could lend a hand,
Attend to them depite their fears.
Just the sound of their voice comes soothe and reassure
Those lonely souls that has captured
This deadly bug with iron fists.
The monster caught off guard, within its vile cloister,
Shivers like the devil, when the Lord, his Master
Showed up in hell as sheer tourist!

Of the cold pestilence they get a closer look,
To decipher the code at their risks and perils.
With a most daring art they go study the spook,
Or in death to them it's revealed.
If they assist in vain, their prayers do console.
From sufferings they soothe their soul
And the Heavens gives their blessings.
If this somber battle leads them to Charon's arms,
Their voice down to the end, soothes with a divine charm
The martyr's untimely passing!

You mortal bon vivants, you nothing can attain,
You who subjugate death, daily taking its blows.
As they look up to you, if the crowd dares complain,
I follow you in deep sorrow.
Unfortunate! Never. Rather willful victim!
The earth I'll never get to screen
Against any devouring scourge,
Neither will I, easing their deadly martyrdom,
Pour friendship and prayers in their worn out bosom
When from their torture they submerge!

Can I offer myself for my brethren as well?
Where are they, the oppressed, where are they, the hangmen?
What scaffold of honor, what sudden ring of knell
Announce the heroes last amen?
While crushing my body, let the tearing torture,
On the cross, to my thirst endured,
Offers the drink of bitter gall.
Content and proud O Lord, I will sing your praises.
The angel of martyrs their soul to You raises
And to Heaven carries them all.

She

Meanwhile, in the crowd I stood,
Meanwhile she stood at my side.
She unveiled an eager mood,
I trembled deep down inside.

The eve blew a gentle breeze,
The crowd cheered the playing game.
Two lovebirds offered a tease,
I kept silent just the same.

And her team won the first set
Her eyes glowed in silent cheer.
I waved at a pal and yet
She idled, willing and near.

I was fourteen and so shy,
She was fifteen and so prone.
The second set flew right by,
Her team won and her joy shone.

She lovely, queen of her class,
I, dorky, still prime teenage.
She disposed to heed my pass,
I, too novice on this stage.

And the lovebirds silent preach
Grew solid in the meanwhile.
The crowd clapped its joy at each
Volley serve given in style.

And she turned to me and smiled
In muted invitation.
In her eyes there was no vile
Or misguided intention.

Deep inside I felt so lost
In a mix of emotions;
The doom I fell in, almost,
And a surging elation.

She was beautiful and slim,
Had the whole world at her feet.
"Till we meet again, it seems"
But she died ... the short of it.

Regrets

Once upon in lifetime, as though to prove a point,
That the power of love still befalls the conjoint,
Two souls gladly surfing over this world meadows,
Hand in hand, relieving one another's sorrow,

Glowing in blissful might, gleaming of the same light,
Emanating a sun, forever warm and bright,
Living one and the same, basking in sweet glory,
Dazzled, like exiting some enchanted story,

Where this pair of lovebirds, with borrowed rays of sun,
Would, in their ecstasy, the rest of us just shun.
If ever they would be, from themselves drawn apart,
They'd resourcefully steer towards their counterpart

And in a sweet sudden, daring the daunting crowd,
Dash towards the other, then soar above the clouds…

Oh yes, I once had known the true love of my life.
I dream of her embrace, so often and so true.
And at the crack of dawn, despite my fiercest strife,
She'd fly, leaving me her sweet dew.

I yearn for her return, down some flowery trail.
I send silent clamors, on my knees, night and day.
But when I hear the knock, sadly it never fails,
To be just a mirage that'd stray.

And if in my weakness I were to let them in,
That would be, of my time, such a waste and a lost.
I'd pay for my beloved, with regrets deep within.
But remorse has a higher cost.

Don't call her name to me, don't rekindle the flame.
Don't speak of this old time when I was once complete,
For the sound of my voice never remains the same,
When I remember my defeat.

Everyone deep inside harbors within their soul,
A lost love and so learned to stifle the deep sighs.
We all carry a cross, paying subtly a toll,
Once our chance has passed us by.

This love boat, in lifetime, only once docks your shore
Blessed is the pilgrim it finds keen and ready!
Whenever it departs, much loaded than before,
You suffer your loss already.

We sober silently; we make all kind of deals.
We beg for an encore, a replay of the scene.
But forward, we all go, nothing's at a standstill.
Only the Lord can intervene.

She flew my Tweedy Bird, without leaving a trace
But she sings in my heart at every crack of dawn.
And still at my window I hope to see her face,
Sweetly skipping upon my lawn…

Oh yes, I had once known, the true love of my life.
I dream of her embrace, so often and so true.
At each crack of my dawn, despite my fiercest strife,
I wake up missing her anew.

Spring to Fall

Today sneaked a meek dawn out of the horizon,
From some quiescent sun well-known to this season,
Clamoring autumn's gentleness.
Today comes with its fears, its concerns and its chores.
Today tiptoes on lawns and souls on every shore,
Revealing the season's meekness.

On the deserted banks of rivers of my mind
Where willows stand groggy from dreams they left behind,
Dreams of a warm and shiny sun.
On the deserted banks where souvenirs abound,
The ghosts of yesterday softly come hang around
But of solace deliver none.

Then all the promises lay flat with heavy sighs.
They feel they no longer bear the dew that won't dry,
That time changed the look of its face.
The many promises utttered under the spell,
That look from the fall stand, under dew, not so well,
Of the old bliss now leave no trace.

The hopes of brighter days linger soft, linger still.
On everyone's journey they barge as though instilled,
As fuel for engine of our life.
Tomorrow's hopes that shine at every start of day,
Calling us to come soothe from deceit done in May,
Source of each other's every strife.

Outrage

*The most vile agression that from a man could come
Would be to strangle France or to go slaughter Rome.
It's from every country, every city or town,
To steal the soul of men, and their freedom to drown.*

*In the sacred chamber, step right in with the sword,
Slit the throats of all laws without any foreword.
Shackle generations would be a vicious crime
That God, calm and serene, would recall for long time.*

*Causing such infamy all graces would withdraw
And the retribution coming slow, coming raw
From Heavens would come down, just as calm and serene
With its whip of brass nails, ready to leave its screen.*

Foolish Mind

Foolish and so unwise can at times be the mind
Trying, in realm of love, some clear answer to find.
This is an exercise in blunt futility,
It meanders far away from its propensity.

The mind is rational, ponders and then decides.
The mind makes decisions on what it has inside.
The mind fickled at times, it's a God-given right,
Shilly-shallies often, idling with all its might.

But the heart, oh the heart, has a mind of its own.
It folllows the blessings that the spirit has thrown.
All comes to it slowly, permeates its fibers,
There it reflects truly the great light it harbors.

There ensues a battle; love goes against reason.
The outcome is always seen throughout every season.
The heart never concedes to the mind the last word.
All gets bloody inside where words go against swords.

But through every season, across every frontier,
The world over, the heart has always shed its tears
As the mind dumfounded, lost in a maze of thoughts,
Is led by a strong leash where the heart is now caught.

Madam

Madam, yes I once thought that the look in your eyes,
Though so gentle, softly did cut me down to size.
I felt small, I fell weak, facing your poise so calm
And this first encounter fed me a silent qualm.

Madam, I swear to God, I would keep it all in.
Entertain this feeling I would do by no mean.
Way out of my league was where I first saw you
And, for the life of me, I never thought it through.

But Madam, with us life plays it tricks sneakily.
Madam, one can never fathom how stealthily
Love can spring in the heart. This the world still baffles.
Right then my heart and mind fell in silent scuffle.

Madam, I had promised not to ever return,
Traipse on fields such as these with fresh wounds that still burn,
But as I said Madam, one truly never knows,
As you tread on the earth, the source of one's sorrow.

I hope so much, Madam, that lost deep in this maze,
That yearning for you hand, you're of me as amazed.
And that you see in me, as I now see in you,
A balm for my torments, my soul most soothing dew.

But Madam I promise not to perturb your peace.
I can't say that at this I am yet a novice.
This way, away from you, this love I will go purge
Even crush this poor heart for allowing this surge.

Madam then rest assured, in no way I had meant,
Your peace and steady life, with my words, to torment.
But love has its reasons which reason do eclipse
But this sweet bind of mine will stay sealed with my lips.

Madam I bid farewell to your loving brown eyes
In which I thought I saw love spring with no disguise.
But often what you miss comes as lovely mirage
When a starved, lonely heart, picks mate without triage.

A Visual

--Hey, trails where are the grass willows,
Wooden meadows, Hills and valleys?
Why this dirge in somber solo?
--He who played doesn't come lately.

--Why no one hangs at your window,
Not a flower in your garden,
Say, house where did your owner go?
--Don't know. He left in a sudden.

--Dog, watch the house. —Why so, why so?
No one lives here as you can see
--Child why you're crying? —I don't know.
--Girl, who you miss? —My fiancee.

--Where did he go? --Where no one goes.
--Waves over reefs topsy-turvying,
Where are you from? —From hell, who knows.
--What do you bring then? A coffin.

The Dawn

Over the somber plain spreads a subtle shiver.
It's time now to get off riding the dream weaver
Or under the twilight, tallying stars so bright,
And separating sheep from rams all through the night.

In horror some of us arise from pleasant dreams.
A furrowed waterfall, catching the first sunbeams,
Glows like a satin drape from this folded mountain.
From the bleak horizon, its dawn this land obtains,

Like a smiling bright face with teeth of golden pearls.
So the cows, the blackbirds and the jays of this world,
And bullfinches alike throw tunes into the woods
Where you can faintly hear voicing the rising brood.

From the fleeting shadow, surging from the haystacks,
The sheep fleece comes bouncing, brightly lining their back,
And the sleepy young girl, from just one eye peeping,
Fresh awaken disrobes, shedding night covering,

As with one foot she looks for her chinese slipper…
Glory then to our God, of all lives the Keeper!
His nature comes to life, subtly and peacefully,
Every given morning, at the same time, surely.

The sun golden arrows pierce the woods canopy
To display to the eyes last day's carbon copy.
It brings warmth, it brings life, brings us a clear message:
The Father's steady Love comes down from age to age.

Ponderings

Whenever come tolling for you
The somber bells that see one through,
Will you, my soul wail and lament
As you traverse this sad moment?

Disregard the queries of this mysterious theme,
Telling of the true Source from where the bright light beams,
For swaddled up in Love, faith will bring you to GOD,
HE who summons all souls to leave the carnal pod.

Fly peacefully towards this ineffable bliss,
Shun the prosper you are, shun whatever you'll miss.
Fly, fly and leave this earth and its puerile fable,
A short tale quickly read, quickly rejectable.

One day we come to watch on life gimongus screen
Between good and evil the eternal fight scenes.
A never ending duel lie-fecundated hate
Does against blessèd Truth; world most heated debate.

The thrill of life itself makes one yearn for the light
Next to the cheap bling-bling of this earth that's so bright.
Like snow on mountain tops, hearts melt in ecstasy
Bathing under the rays warming the seven seas.

Facing the creation, the creature asks proudly:
"What is your origin, you who springs so boldly"?
Are you work of the Hand that makes tremble the just?"
But from asking in vain, his stance he readjusts.

As he ponders this way his heart only love, brings.
Love whose blessèd meaning loudly spells sufferings.
Since the dawning of age, this rigid equation
Finds its serene balance in our every action.

You'll witness suffering and you, yourself will bleed
And will shed many tears till you doubt your own creed.
Misery has branded this so vast universe,
Its echo in all hearts resonates in reverse.

The only true meaning of this fleeting sojourn
That we spend on this earth, the meaning of its bourne
Rings out love of brethren, its outmost expression.
Charity transpires when love is in action.

This golden spark of Love who brought us charity
Came and lived in our midst, straight from the Trinity.
To humans He's offered as treasured guiding light
As a way back to God, making all darkness bright.

My soul you will suffer, mostly if from the flame
Of love consuming you, you once poor and once lame,
You'll have failed to entice any other brethren
Or move other soul mates to sing the same refrain.

Chances are in your life you will have only met
With cold hearted brethren whom your flame could not melt.
If from roses you held all you could feel were thorns,
Keep going on your way, your bleeding hands don't mourn.

Go ahead with your task, that's to you the wise choice.
Aspire to the Truth, to everything God voiced.
Don't doubt the outcome at the end of the times,
Know that the final Juge is still the great I AM.

Tears were shed joyfully at your very first dawn,
Tears will be shed throughout your life upon this lawn,
In this valley of tears were nothing's here to last,
Tears and more tears will fall when your days here have passed.

Know that this loud chaos that the whole world, scrambles
Is fed by the Spirit of God that enables.
That created from love, nature's bound to suffer,
That we have one True God whose life is still offered.

As from an exile full of grief,
Fly my soul to divine relief.
Don't regret the joys of this sphere
When the time comes to fly from here.

Milton Keynes UK
Ingram Content Group UK Ltd.
UKHW041953291124
451915UK00001B/183